The
BOOK
of
COELIUS

ISBN 978 1 907881 20 6

The publisher wishes to thank Christopher Warnock & John
Michael Greer for their kind permission to reprint their
translations from the *Picatrix*.

www.hadeanpress.com

THE
BOOK
OF
COELIUS

WRITTEN BY ALCHEMIST
CHRISTOPHER BRADFORD
AETHERIUS INTRA TERRA

KAMEOTHIC INTERNAL ALCHEMY

TRAINING MANUAL FOR THE
ORDO OCTOPI NIGRI PULVERI

TABLE OF CONTENTS

Introduction	9
Purpose – Accomplishing the Great Work	11
Learning the Language of the Birds	13
The Alchemical Forces	23
The Use of Hebrew within the Ordo	25
The Four Worlds	27
The Symbols of the Ordo	29
The Alchemical Dragon	29
Our Alchemical Process	33
The Process	34
Method – The Ritual Structure and Practice	37
Ordo Octopi Nigri Pulveri	37
Rites and Ritual Components	39
Ritual Organization – Our Golden Dawn Heritage	39
The Kamea	39
On the *Picatrix*	40
The Altar Setup	40
The Sign of the Enterer	40
The Sign of Silence	41
The Bellows Breath	42
Moving the Awareness	43
The Solar Cross Ritual	44
Purification Rituals	47
The Ablution with Holy Water	47
The Banishing of Uninvited Spirits	47
The Angelic Summoning Rite	48
Creating the Tower of Art	48

Calcination, Sublimation and Coagulation Rituals 53
The Holy Yeheshua Rite 53
The Prayer of the Gnomes (EARTH) 56
The Prayer of the Undines (WATER) 56
The Prayer of the Sylphs (AIR) 57
The Prayer of the Salamanders (FIRE) 58
Mudra 60
The Qabalistic Cross 62
The Lemnian Fire Rite 65
Some Further Notes on the Alchemical Body 68
The Antimaquis Rite 69
The Planetary Incantations 74
Dissolution and Putrefication 79
The Death Litany 79
The Death Rite of Saturn 80
The Book of The Blossoming Flower 87
Theory and Method 89
Spagery 89
The Garden 90
The Spagyrist's Tools 91
Spagyric Alchemical Symbols 93
The Spagyric Alchemical Process 94
Process and Products 97
Making a Spagyric Tincture 97
Making Spagyric Oils 99
Making Spagyric Elixirs 99
Creating the Unda Superum 103
Scrying the Unda Superum 104
The Art of Spagyric Healing 105
Treating at the Physical level – Basic Herbalism 105
General Chart for Treating common Physical Ailments 106
Treating Personality Issues 107
How to create a Poultice 107
The Tools of the Alchemical Healer 109
The Staff of Imhotep 109
Consecrating the Staff of Imhotep 110

The Book of Images   110
The Rites of Healing   111
The Ritual of Adoration   112
The Ritual of Healing   113
The Act of Thanksgiving   114
Practical Applications of the Holy Yeheshua Rite   115
Creating Servant Spirits   115
Invoking the Astrological Forces   116
The Twelve Banners Rite   119
The Magic of the Decans   121
The Healing Magic of the Decans   121
Opening the Temple   122
Creating the Triangle   122
Creating the Circle   123
The Process   124
The *Testament* excerpt, with Planetary Rulers and the Banners used to Summon the Decan Spirits   124
For Further Alchemical Understanding – an analysis of Philalethes' *Font of Chemical Truth* from the perspective of the Ordo Octopi Nigri Pulveri   135

INTRODUCTION

THIS WORK IS A DISTILLATION OF CEREMONIAL AND ALCHEMICAL MAGIC WITH African-American Conjure Magic. My aim with this small work is to present a system of practical Internal Alchemy, rooted in the Western Hermetic Tradition. In our system we work to refine the Prima Materia from the inside-out, and from the outside-in. The practical methods of Hoodoo conjure magic paired with Spagyric Alchemy are key to creating change in our external world and working upon the person from the Outside-In. This system utilizes Bardonian-Hermetic Inner Alchemical methods with deep roots in the Golden Dawn (the school within which I learned the Art of Magic and Alchemy) for working from the Inside-Out, and is meant to support the Magical life and enable a daily magical practice that breathes in time to the rhythms of our cosmos. This isn't a scholarly work; I won't be providing you with reams of sources and the like. It is a work about developing a useful alchemical practice.

I've used methods that are publicly available – if one has the eyes to see – so that no tradition is profaned with the publication of this manual. My vows preclude me from including any material I've been given that directly speaks to the methods of other Organizations; having learned how Alchemical processing works, I've put together a spiritual practice that accomplishes the goal of the Great Work without revealing the exact processing system of other traditions. This system pulls from the traditions I have been trained in, without appropriating directly their full method.

So, this is a new tradition, and I make no claims to grand lineage for this particular system, as it has roots in antiquity but begins practically with me and my brothers in the Ordo Octopi. I do have direct transmission from living Alchemical Masters, and have received training from them in the continental Golden Dawn and Great Rite traditions. What you receive here is a flower sprung from that soil, but certainly not the same thing.

Gentlefolk who wish to join our fellowship may do so by contacting the current head of the Ordo Octopi Nigri Pulveri via the publisher.

PURPOSE: ACCOMPLISHING THE GREAT WORK

THE GOAL OF THE GREAT WORK IS TO TRANSMUTE THE LEAD OF OUR MATERIAL selves into the Gold of a fully realized spiritual nature. This isn't a purely spiritual transformation, but is a change in the physical and spiritual natures of the Alchemist. All Matter is Spirit, and all Spirit is Matter; they differ only in coagulation.

This process is continual. Kameothic Internal Alchemy is a lifestyle, not a part-time practice. It will permeate throughout your life, and the Gold that you reap in evolving and altering yourself will apply on all levels: personal, physical, spiritual, emotional. Understanding of how the process works upon us at all levels can be had by studying and meditating upon the Hermetic Axiom.

"That which is above is like unto that which is below, and that which is below is like unto that which is above, to accomplish the Miracle of the One Thing." (Summarized, Hermes Thrice-Greatest.)

We continually return to the Hermetic Axiom, because the truth of the First Matter – the One Matter, the Azoth – is held within it. Gnosis, true understanding of this, is experiential and not a matter of the intellect. I will tell you exactly what it is, and you will come to know it yourself during the Alchemical work, likely during the Putrefaction process. It must be held to be known.

Understand that accomplishing the Great Work does not mean annihilation of the personality as it does in some Eastern methods. In our way, our aim is to refine the individual Soul so that it is, in fact, Immortal, and not ever-dying and being reborn. For this to occur, the seed of Soul that is the root of each being must be encouraged to sprout and grow. During each incarnation Nature applies a bit of heat to the Seed. It would, eventually, sprout a fully grown soul on its own. Our aim is to lend nature a hand, so that the process may be completed in a single lifetime.

LEARNING THE LANGUAGE OF THE BIRDS

ALCHEMICAL GLOSSARY

IN ORDER TO UNDERSTAND THE LANGUAGE OF ALCHEMY, ONE MUST HAVE AN internally consistent set of definitions for the terminology found within Alchemical manuscripts. There are many, many different interpretations for the different terms used in Alchemy. The key to understanding is that the terms need to be consistent within the system that you are using. They should be so deeply ingrained that when the Alchemist reads a manuscript by even a practitioner of a different Alchemical path, the meanings leap off of the page, and the process is understood.

The following are the definitions of some common Alchemical terms as they are understood within the Kameothic Internal Alchemical system; other systems may have different definitions, but these are the definitions that must be internalized if we are to properly understand this system that we practice. They should be read and internalized, and the Alchemist should go and analyze alchemical manuscripts with these understandings in mind; this will build a consistent set of internal correspondences. At the end of this manuscript is a short and quick analysis of the *Font of Chemical Truth* by Philalethes, using this method, as an example of how having an internally consistent set of correspondences can help build understanding of Alchemy and the Alchemical language.

Air – a manifestation of the Higher Consciousness, of Mercury. The Etheric body and Aura.

Azoth – the source of all being, the sea of mind, God. The One thing.

Birds – refers to grace descending from heaven (as when the Seed of Soul within the person enters the Lunar Body, making it pregnant with the Crowned Child). Also refers to the Inner Fires, the sublimation of internal virtue. Birds are things that "fly", that ascend into the Heavens and return to the Earth. We see in the movement of the Inner Fires this same motion; the fires rise into the Head (heaven) and then coagulate and permeate the entire body (descending back to Earth).

Black Powder – the self-awareness reduced to Azoth/Chaos, the blackness made up of innumerable individual "grains" (souls). This is also a perception of the spiritual body of God. This is a state of being, the state of the Alchemist after he has confronted and been consumed by the Death-Force personified by the titan Saturn.

Chaos – the root state, the undifferentiated nature of the Source. The Black Powder.

Cinnabar Fields – these are large pools of Inner Virtue in the body, from which the Metals draw their life. There are three of them: one in the Navel; another surrounding the area of the Heart; and one within the Head.

Decay/Rot/Putrefy – The destruction of an image when it is meditated upon... it loses its outward appearance and reveals its inner Nature. At first this appears to be nothing but Blackness... further meditation (which is surrounding the object in our Philosophical Mercury) reveals this blackness to be alive, with throbbing points of light. This blackness is the Azoth, the substance of all things and the flesh of God. When we turn the power of Dissolution upon ourselves, we enter into putrefaction which is, among other things, the contemplation and understanding of Death. This comes with the rising of the Saturnian force, which destroys the Fixity of the Salt-force within the person, enabling direct experience of the Infinite for the Alchemist.

Disrobing Woman – a symbol of Nature revealing herself to the Alchemist.

Dragons/Serpents – internal fires, sometimes related to the Desire-force in the Mars center, sometimes the Death Force in the Saturn center, and sometimes – especially when there is an Ouroboros – to the circulation of the internal Fires. Very often relates to a particular upwelling of the internal forces. The Earth Dragon held within the lower Cinnabar field in particular is often symbolized by a winged Dragon with two legs.

Dryness – this relates to the manifested solidity of a thing. The "dry" qualities of the Matured Sulfur are its entrenchment in physicality.

Earth – The physical body, also "Lemnian Earth". Lemnian is a reference to the god Vulcan, whose forge was in Lemnos. So, "Fiery Earth" refers also to our furnace. This is a manifestation of the Salt principle, the Body. Also refers to Elemental Earth.

Eagle – a subtle exhalation, or "Vapor", so-called because it rises into the "heavens", the head. Also a symbol of the volatile, of the spiritual nature, which isn't crystallized – isn't fixed – in the same way the physical nature is due to the operation of the Alchemical Salt.

Fire – a manifestation of the Solar/Active consciousness, also the Desire-Force and Concentration/Attention. Also alludes to the Vapor that wells forth from calcined Metals, Inner Fire.

First Matter – this is the Azoth. Often, when referenced in alchemical literature, it can be an allusion to the Prima Materia as well.

Furnace – The Physical Body, made of "clay", of Earth, which bears within it a transforming fire.

Gold – the super-consciousness and Soul, and the refined substance of Azoth and of Mercury. The masculine counterpart to the feminine Silver. Also refers to the Solar energies within the body. This force is often perceived and colored Red in the old manuscripts.

Hermaphrodite – this is the result of the Sublimation/Coagulation cycle. The **Rebis**, where the "Flying" refined spiritual Nature is joined to the "Fixed" physical Nature. This Vapor is released by the Calcination of the Metals, and then Coagulated back into the body. It is an Inner Fire, and is referred to as Amrita and Manna in other traditions, when it condenses and pervades the physical body. The Hermaphrodite is the combination of two separate things with the same fundamental nature. This is the Alchemist who has raised and joined the Solar and Lunar forces within himself.

Jupiter (Tin) – The Solar Plexus, expressed just beneath the ribs at the center of the Torso.

Lato – the mind/soul of the Alchemist.

Lions – also refer to the Inner Fires.

Luna (Silver) – Pituitary Gland, expressed between the Eyes.

Mars (Iron) – The Perenial Nerves, expressed just below the Navel and within the sexual organs.

Mercury – Mind/Spirit. The Metals are but "fixed" mercury, which is Mercury concentrated and made semi-Solid. Mercury taking on a different form depending upon which plane it operates. (See the Qabalistic Four Worlds). Thus, the metals themselves are made up of Mercury, and are dissolved in Mercury and refined by Mercury. All is Mind, and there is no fundamental difference between Matter and Spirit; they are the same thing. Matter is simply Spirit coagulated.

Mercury (the Planet/Interior Star Mercury) – Pineal Gland, expressed at the top of the head.

Mineral Water – mind/spirit with awakened Inner Metals/Planets. The awakened Etheric body. The Green Lion.

Moon – the Sub-conscious Mind, the deep female mind, the hidden mind. The Etheric body. The Woman. The automated mind that powers the Waking, Male mind and runs the furnace of the body. The Natural fire of digestion is addressed through work with the Moon (this comes from P.F. Case). Also refers to the Lunar current of inner Fire within the body.

Mountains – the Body of the Alchemist.

Natural fire – Digestion, also the Inner fires contained within the Metals and the Cinnabar Fields. This is nerve-force contained within the Centers that rises and descends as the metals become subtle, and are gently heated with the un-natural fire by the breath, awareness, and intent of the Alchemist.

Rain Water – water from Heaven, Soul. Different from the common "Water" Mercury, which is the Mind. This is Mercury infused with the Solar virtue, with Gold.

Red Ore – Matured Sulfur, the Physical Body, the refined Desire-Force of the Alchemist, located in the Mars Center. Also the Conscious Mind which is the Sun, and the Red King; the two are inextricably linked. The desire-force is fundamental to shaping the personality. The Mind and its fire is the Red Ore.

We have to understand the Prima Materia as a series of more and less coagulated emanations of the Soul. The Soul emanates the Spirit, from which the Body is emanated. The Mind is a subtle emanation of the Body; it rises from the body like the vaporous clouds that rise from the earth and sea of our macrocosmic World.

Salt – The Physical Body, the Principle of Coagulation and solidity. Manifestation.

Saltpeter – this is the refined physical Body of the Alchemist, the stone part of the Philosopher's Stone. Translated, it literally means "Stone Salt". The "Water" of Saltpeter is the refined Mercury, the gold-infused mind that has grown within it a Soul. The refined "stone" emanates a mind/spirit-body that is of the same quality itself has attained.

Saturn (the Planet/Interior Star Lead) – The Sacral nerves at the base of the Spine, expressed at the Perineum.

Silver – the refined sub-consciousness, the Spirit. The reflection of the Sun, also the Lunar energies within the body. These are White.

Springs – alludes to the welling forth of the Inner Fires from their hidden places within the body (usually the nerve-centers that we call the Metals and Planets, or the Cinnabar Fields).

Sulfur – The Desire nature, the Sexual Energies, The Creative force, the true Fire with which we expand and emanate.

Sun - the Soul-seed, and the Waking Mind/personality. This personality is an emanation of the body which is itself an emanation of the Soul-seed (through the Spirit) that we contain within us.

Unrefined the personality is "gross", as is the body that emanated it. When the body has been refined and made subtle by the Alchemical process, it emanates a personality/Self that is infused with the multiplied essence of the Soul-seed, with Gold, and becomes immortal. This immortality is freedom from endless rebirth - the sprouting of the seed - and is not purely physical immortality.

Sun (the Planet/Interior Star Gold) - The Cardiac Nerve Center, expressed above the Heart.

The Black Stone/Powder - the Mind with personality destroyed/ground to dust by Saturn, and then reborn. The Alchemist who has confronted the Death-Force. The Alchemist who is in deep and sustained meditation, the product of putrefaction.

The Crowned Child - this is the Soul, once a seed at the root of being, Multiplying throughout the Bodies of the Alchemist. The Crowned Child is the Alchemist who's been blessed with a Soul, and not just the seed of Soul that all things are born with. The Soul is gestated in the Spiritual Body, and eventually is "born" into the World of the physical Body.

The Elixir - The Philosopher's Stone.

The Green Lion - The physical body of the Alchemist after the Mineral Water has been created; this is after some Sublimation and Coagulation has occurred. Images of the Green Lion consuming the Sun are showing the refined alchemical body internalizing the Solar Nature. This is equivalent to the Incineration phase.

The King - The Solar Consciousness, Active (the Waking mind). The King has rulership over the Bodies.

The Metals - The nerve-centers within the Body and their expressions in the Subtle bodies. They are the Seven Planets of magical lore and the Interior Stars.

The Miner – the Alchemist.

The Philosopher's Stone – is the refined and subtle Mind of the Alchemist, and is also the refined and subtle Body of the Alchemist; these things are not separate, but are one thing. The Rebis will have been long acquired by the time the Stone is created. It also refers to the Azoth, and the unity of all things. It is a state of being.

The Queen – She is the Lunar Consciousness, and the hidden force which governs the body and dreams. The Queen is the Spirit. She is the Moon to the King's Sun.

The Red Lion – also the Red Stone, the Body of the completed Great Work. The Adept has accomplished the evolution of his body, and need not fear death.

The Red Stone/Powder – the Solar seed that was planted during the Incineration phase (creating the White stone, after steady Calcination) sprouts. The Crowned Child is born, and the Multiplication phase begins. This is the completion of the Great Work.

The Rose – the heavenly and refined Mind

The Seed of Metals – The golden essence contained within the unrefined nerve/energetic centers within the Body, released as Vapor during Calcination. When refined to purity, the metals are like a Salamander, impervious to fires.

The Three-Headed Bird – also the White Stone, the Alchemist who has undergone Calcination, and unified the King (the Mind and Body), the Queen (The Spirit), and the Son (the Soul). He now perceives the three forces that make up existence. (Mercury, Salt, Sulfur).

The White Stone/Powder – The Alchemist who has received the Seed of Soul from heaven. This happens after the Putrefication experience is had, after the Alchemist attains the Black Powder and performs still more calcining upon the Prima Materia. The White stone is attained when the Heavens bring the Mind and the Spirit into Union.

The World – the physical Body, also a reference to the Macrocosm.

Toad – a symbol of the fixed, and also of the physical body.

Triple Fire – The Inner Fires of the Metals, the Un-natural fire, and the digestive Fire.

Two Headed Dragon – the Manna, LVX, the internal Fires within the body. It differentiates into the Lunar and Solar currents, making it "two-headed".

Un-natural fire – the LVX, the hidden fire within breath, the subtle energy that pervades the cosmos. Called Un-natural because it is brought into the Alchemist's Sphere from the Macrocosm, as opposed to the Inner Fires that are "naturally" held within the Alchemist's body.

Venus (Planet/Interior star/Bronze) – The Throat/Lymph Glands, expressed at the Throat.

Vessel – the Sphere of Sensation/Aura – it is made of "glass", a transparent vessel.

Viscous Solid – a flowing solid; the Matured Sulfur after "digestion", which is application of gentle heat with the un-natural fire. This is the subtle-making of the physical body and personality by filling them with LVX. It must be understood that the personality rules directly over the physical body, as the King, and so what happens in one is reflected in the other. See the Hermetic Axiom. The calcination has turned it into a powder (so-called because a powder, although still dry, is malleable and can better absorb and blend with liquid... like the Mercurial Water) and the Mercury has become joined to it wholly. Then the two, which are actually One, but in different states of "Dryness" or Coagulation, can be joined while retaining some of their separate qualities, creating the Hermaphrodite.

Water – the Spirit, Meditation, Mercury. Spirit and sometimes the deep Mind, depending upon context.

White Ore – Water/Undigested Mercury – the Spirit of the Alchemist. Also the Sub-conscious Mind; the two are inextricably linked. The Sub-conscious mind is the Moon and the White Queen, and directly expresses the Spiritual body.

THE ALCHEMICAL FORCES

EXISTENCE IS A BALANCED INTERACTION BETWEEN THREE FUNDAMENTAL Alchemical Forces: the Salt force, the Sulfur force, and the Mercurial force.

Alchemical Salt: This is the limiting force, the Solidifying force, the coagulating force, the force that creates the illusion of the separation of things. As the mineral Salt is crystalline, so too does the Salt force crystallize the spiritual, so that it becomes tangible and Material. The Salt force is the Body of the World. This is important to understand; the physical bodies that the material realm is composed of are all condensed spirituality. There is no real difference between matter and Spirit; the perceived difference is the work of the Salt force.

Alchemical Sulfur: This is the invigorating force, the Fire of the soul, the Desire nature that fuels chemical change in the Mineral kingdom, growth in the Vegetable kingdom, pro-creation in the Animal kingdom, and all of these things in addition to the Creative impulse within the Alchemical Man. It is the focused will of the Red King, the fire behind the personality that rules the body like a tyrant.

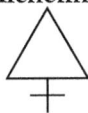

Alchemical Mercury: This is the communicative force, the interpenetrating force, the Water of the soul. It is the fluid within which all things are suspended. It is the Mother of all things, and carries them within her Womb. Sulfur and Salt are both within her, and Sulfur acts upon Salt only through the medium of Mercury.

The interaction of these forces in the Macrocosm creates the Universe, and within the Microcosm creates us all. Understand that in Alchemy One thing is many things; each of these forces has a different manifestation on different levels of being, both internally and externally to the Alchemical Adept. In order for the process to make sense, we have to grasp the Nature of the First Matter and understand how it changes and permeates itself through the various worlds.

THE USE OF HEBREW WITHIN THE ORDO

Teit	Cheit	Zayin	Vav	Hei	Dalet	Gimel	Beit	Alef
(T)	(Ch)	(Z)	(V/O/U)	(H)	(D)	(G)	(B/V)	(Silent)

Samekh	Nun	Nun	Mem	Mem	Lamed	Khaf	Kaf	Yod
(S)	(N)	(N)	(M)	(M)	(L)	(Kh)	(K/Kh)	(Y)

Tav	Shin	Reish	Qof	Tzadei	Tzadei	Fe	Pei	Ayin
(T/S)	(Sh/S)	(R)	(Q)	(Tz)	(Tz)	(F)	(P/F)	(Silent)

HEBREW HAS A LENGTHY HISTORY WITHIN THE WESTERN ESOTERIC TRADITION as an excellent magical script and language; the Hebrew we use is not the same as the spoken language. Each letter has certain esoteric meanings, and vibration of the letters can be used to great effect. The nature of the Hebrew alphabet – which gives numerical meanings in addition to sounds for each letter – is such that it is a perfect vehicle for carrying occult meaning and power. Qabalistic study is thoroughly encouraged for our members. A short treatise on the Qabalah written by Eliphas Levi called *Elements of the Qabalah* is a fantastic introduction.

THE FOUR WORLDS

Western Alchemical Traditions (of which this is now one) are interpenetrated with Qabalistic understanding of the nature of Existence. The perspectives are not always exactly the same, but the fundamental truths are. The understanding of the Four Worlds is one of those fundamental understandings necessary to working within this tradition and to grasping the Alchemical process.

Yod/Atziluth/Fire: Yod is the Hebrew Letter for Fire, and is also representative of Atziluth. This is the realm of first causes, of Sulfur and of Soul. It is the spark of fire that precedes action, a realm of formlessness and pure being. This is a realm that coincides with Alchemical Sulfur.

In the Microcosm, this is the seed of Soul, the purely spiritual Gold that is the beginning and root of a being.

Heh (blue)/Briah/Water: Heh is the Hebrew Letter for Water (it is also the Hebrew letter for Earth, which is the coagulation of the other Elements. This is rooted in the mystery of Birth and the Black Mother Binah, which comes from study of the Tree of Life. We see this first, watery Heh as Blue, and the Earthly Heh as Black.) and is the Spirit and the realm where things are given the structure that becomes form in Assiah. It is here that ideas/beings gestate. The root is in Yod/Atziluth, which grows into Heh/Briah and impregnates her. It is given form – "Clothing" – in Vau/Yetzirah which is the realm of images, and is birthed/given Being in Heh/Assiah. This process is both Macrocosmic and Microcosmic, and is also known as the **Path of Manifestation**.

This is the realm of Emotion, where things are not visualized but felt and perceived through awareness. The realm of emotion is closer to fundamental reality than that of intellect, which is why oftentimes the power of emotion can override the sensibility of the intellect for persons in whom the water element is strong. Within the Microcosm this is the deep Mind, the sub-conscious mind. This is a realm that coincides with Alchemical Mercury in this system.

Vau/Yetzirah/Air: Vau is the Hebrew letter for Air and also representative of the plane of Yetzirah. This is the realm of images, where things are clothed in appearance, the Astral realm. This realm is interpenetrated by Briah, and interpenetrates her as well.

In the Microcosm this is the Sphere of Sensation, and also the Waking mind and intellect. It is both Alchemical Mercury and Alchemical Sulfur.

Heh (black)/Assiah/Earth: Heh (final) is the Hebrew Letter for Earth and also for Assiah. Assiah is the realm of solidity, of crystallization. It is composed of the crystallized spirituality of the aforementioned worlds. It contains all of the Worlds and all of their substances, and manifests them in physicality. This is the realm of the Alchemical Salt Force, where it is dominant. This realm is also composed of Alchemical Mercury and Alchemical Sulfur; here, they are primarily expressed through Alchemical Salt as their natures are crystallized.

In the Microcosm, this is the Alchemical Furnace, the Physical Body, which is composed of dense matter, the Etheric body, the Mind and the Soul. The World that is the Alchemist. In Assiah, we have all of the other Worlds contained and crystallized into Form. This is why Man, as the Microcosm, is a reflection of God, who is the Macrocosm.

This is by no means an exhaustive and definitive text on the Four Worlds. Outside study is necessary to supplement the understanding.

THE SYMBOLS OF THE ORDO

THE NAME OF THIS SATURNIAN ORDER IS INTENTIONALLY SOMEWHAT outlandish and also completely accurate symbolically. The symbolism of the Octopi within the order is very useful in describing the Alchemical Work we do (as a creature that lives in the depths of the Sea, much the same as the golden Child we wish born within ourselves), as we divide the work of Alchemy into 8 stages, and require mastery of 8 particular magical arts for one to join our ranks as an Alchemical Adept. Attainment of the Black Powder state is the line separating Alchemical Adepts from Aspirants, and so the Black Octopus is the symbol of the Alchemical Adepts of this Order.

THE ALCHEMICAL DRAGON

OUR SYMBOL IS THE CLASSIC DRAWING OF AZOTH, THE ALCHEMICAL DRAGON. Azoth's parts and image symbolize the Unity of the One while also delineating its disparate parts.

The Dragon has the scaly body of a Serpent, which as a creature that slithers upon the ground is a symbol of Earth and the Physical, and of things rooted in the Earth. It also, however, bears wings and the winged feet of Mercury, which are a symbol of the Spiritual. So, the Alchemical Dragon is an entity that is both physical and spiritual in nature. It bears a human head in its belly, with a beard that symbolizes Wisdom and Angelic wings for ears, which symbolize the Heavens. The head itself is Consciousness, and shows that our Alchemical Dragon is no wild beast, but is at the very core a thing of consciousness. Nature isn't a blind thing.

Atop the neck we find three heads. One of which is a Crescent Moon, illuminated before and behind by the Sun (symbolized by the head of a Phoenix). This alludes to the Moon being a reflection of the Sun and drawing her light from it. We know from our studies that the Moon is a symbol of the Etheric Body and the Sub-Conscious Mind. So, we learn that the Moon is enlivened by the Sun, and therefore the Etheric Body is enlivened and powered by the Solar nature that is both the Seed of God and the Spark of Soul within us, and the Physical Body, which is a gross emanation of that very same soul. We come to understand that the Etheric Body is interpenetrated by the Solar nature, and draws sustenance from the Physical Body of the Alchemist. This symbol, of the Moon illuminated afore and behind by the Sun – suggesting the Rebis, the combination of two disparate natures – is suggestive of Matter, which is coagulated Spirit, and a Union of Spirit in its most Gross and most Ethereal natures. This is summed up in the Alchemical symbol of Salt, which is crystalline, the essence of the liquid coagulated into a solid Form. The first head is the Alchemical Salt.

The Second head is that of the Sun and Solar nature, which is marked as the seed of Soul within all things, and also the physical body that is emanated from the soul in order for it to experience materiality. The physical body is composed entirely of Solar Energy, as are all living things upon the Earth. The personality is emanated from the Physical body as a means for the individual Soul to interact with the Outer world. The Desire-Force, which is also the Sexual Force (this is not simply an expression of sexuality, but also that of Need), is the engine that powers the creation of the Personality, which is primarily a reactionary body, built by the outer world's reactions to the expressed needs of the individual Soul and the soul's reactions to the Outer World. All of these things are rooted primarily in the Solar nature, and are symbolized by the Red King, and by the Alchemical Symbol of Sulfur. Understanding Alchemy means understanding the interpenetration of all things; no symbol has one simple meaning in Alchemy, but is made up of layers and layers of connected meaning. The second head is Alchemical Sulfur.

The Third head is that of the Mercurial Nature; it has the shape of the Sun, but the color of the Moon, and bears the cross below which is symbol of the intersection of Spiritual and Physical, and the horns which are the symbol of Nature. The shape of the Sun is an allusion to its fundamentally Solar nature, and the color of the Moon shows that it carries the Solar nature while being a reflection of it. The Mercurial nature is the Mind, which is also an emanation of the Soul, but is most subtle. It is separate from the Personality (and becomes clearly separated by the Alchemical work). It interpenetrates the various bodies, and encompasses them all. The microcosmic mind is a reflection of the Macrocosmic Mind, which is the source of all things. This is Mercury. Everything is the Mercury, and the Mercury is Gold. The third head is Alchemical Mercury.

The tail of the Dragon is knotted firmly about the necks of the Solar and Lunar heads – the heads of Salt and Sulfur – while laying but gently over the neck of the Mercurial head. This is an allusion to the firmness of the grasp materiality has upon those Alchemical Substances, and to the freedom of the Mind to do as it wills. The Mind and the substance of the mind are the key to liberation and transformation.

The Dragon is also a symbol of the Inner Fires, the subtle Vapors that rise from the Internal Metals. These Vapors rise by the work of the Mind, which uses the substance of the Physical and Etheric bodies to evolve the nature of the Alchemist.

Within the very image of the Ordo we find the essence of Alchemical understanding in Azoth, which is fundamentally an image representing the God and Source of All. There is no more profound symbol of Alchemy than the Alchemical Dragon Azoth.

A key thing to understand here is that with true and proper understanding of Alchemy, almost any tale or image can be understood in such a way as to reveal Alchemical processes. Alchemy is not just a spiritual practice, it is also a description of the processes of nature and existence, and so all things that depict that process also show the processes of Alchemy.

OUR ALCHEMICAL PROCESS

THERE ARE A NUMBER OF DIFFERENT ALCHEMICAL PROCESSES USED BY THE esoteric traditions of different cultures throughout the ages. They all fundamentally aim to do the same thing – use Mercury to refine the Metals into Gold, and use Gold-infused Mercury to refine the nature of the Alchemist. There are internal and external paths, Dry and Wet and Amalgam ways, and all that are created from an initiated perspective, with true understanding of the Alchemical process, can lead to one accomplishing the Great Work. Our process is written below. It isn't the only process, and is somewhat of an amalgam, but it works. Our inspiration is found in Philalethes, Basil Valentine, Paul Foster Case, Nicolas Flamel and the Alchemical structure of the Golden Dawn. The following is a short explanation of our process; deeper understanding requires study of the works of Philalethes, and meditation upon the emblems and aphorisms in the Hermetic Garden of Daniel Stolices from the perspective of this system. Alchemists have differing interpretations of the meaning behind the work of the famous Alchemists, including Philalethes. He is said by some to be teaching the Dry way of Antimony – the Path of the Black Dragon. This is a perfectly valid interpretation of his works. When seen with the eyes of the Ordo's internal Alchemical system, however, the meaning is different and quite clear. If the Alchemical Adept has properly internalized this system of understanding he will have no difficulty reading alchemical texts and interpreting them in a fashion consistent with it.

This doesn't in any way mean that our understanding of these texts is the key one or the only correct one, but that it is an internally correct view from the perspective of Internal Alchemy. To understand the perspective, study the definitions given in this text for Alchemical figures, and use them to analyze the Alchemical texts of first Philalethes, and then other Alchemical fathers.

A thorough analysis of the Alchemical meanings of various emblems, samples of Spagyric accomplishment and demonstration of Alchemical accomplishment are required for advancement through the few grades of the Ordo Octopi Nigri Pulveri (these are Fridgida, Tepente, and lastly Ardens Solis). They allude to spiritual states. The grade of Fridgida is acquired after some time of practice and passing a test on Spagyrics. After acquiring the grade of Tepente, an initiate has earned the title of "Alchemist". There are three titles which an Alchemist may bear.

◊   The Black
◊   The White
◊   The Red

The titles don't allude to spiritual states; they *are* spiritual states. An Alchemist is referred to by his name and title (should he have one). For example, I'm referred to as Christopher "the White". I was once Christopher the Black, after having attained the Black Powder, and I hope to one day be Christopher the Red. I have managed to Calcine the First Matter into the White state, after years of effort. I hope for my seed of Soul to Multiply and be birthed from my Mercurial Sea; and when it does I'll have earned that title.

THE PROCESS

First, **Purification** of the bodies and Sphere of Sensation, so that our Alchemical vessel is clear of dross when we perform our calcinating meditative work.

Calcination (applying "heat", filling the bodies with LVX) so that the body itself is made "subtle", with the "gross" and heavy elements themselves spiritualized by the LVX. This causes Separation, which we treat as part of the Calcination process in this system.

Sublimation, which is work directly upon the Interior Metals; Calcining them directly causes them to release their vapor (this release of the vapor is sublimation), which is an Eagle in some Metals and a Serpent in others. This alludes to the subtlety of the Vapor, which determines whether its effect is most strongly felt physically or spiritually. This fine vapor is subtle, and works to make us subtle and leads to the next step, which is Coagulation. This Vapor is also an Inner Fire.

Coagulation is the combination of the subtle-making Vapor – which is the Virtue released by the Metals within the body after calcining them

– with the Etheric and Physical bodies of the Alchemist. This alters the nature of the Alchemist, so that he can hold more and more of the subtle LVX as time goes on.

Dissolution occurs during pure meditation, in which we contemplate firstly things outside of ourselves until they dissolve within the Mercury of our Mind, and then contemplate our own Nature until it too dissolves, revealing the reality of Being to us. This is the woman Nature disrobing herself before the Alchemist, unveiling her Secrets. This is also connected with the rising of the Black Serpent, which creates the Black Powder out of our own minds. Often the Alchemist first truly grasps and understands the nature of the First Matter during this practice.

Putrefaction is the contemplation of Death, the vision of all things as impermanent and dying that are "separate" from God. The practical meditation upon the Death-Force leads to a lifting of the Veil of Salt, so that we can see the truth that all things are God and separation but an illusion. In order to do this, we have to immerse ourselves in Death and putrefy right along with it. This is a fundamental stepping-stone for the Alchemist. After this has been accomplished, all that is truly required is steady Calcination of the Body and individual Metals and prayer. This is the Black Phase of the Work.

Incineration is the spark of Gold that is the seed of soul prayed for by the Alchemist growing into the Lunar Self/White Ore/Mercury and impregnating it. Accomplishing this practice requires some austerity and prayerful invocation, in addition to the regular Calcining practice. Here the Alchemy of Food and Water comes into play, as we use dissolution to alter the nature of our Food and make it powerfully Solar. In this way, we make the temple ready at all levels for the indwelling of the Soul. This Phase is the White Phase of the Work.

Multiplication, in which the Seed of Soul is born as the Solar Child and permeates the bodies of the Alchemist, after having been carried in the womb of the Spiritual body and nurtured there during the Incineration. This is an automated step, accomplished by the regular Calcination and meditative work. This Phase is the Red Phase of the Work.

There are other systems that stretch the process out to 12 steps so that it is harmonious with the Zodiac; these usually include more automated processes that are not caused directly by the Will and Work of the Alchemist, being effects that occur because of the regular Calcination (and Separation), Sublimation, Dissolution and Coagulation (sometimes also called Condensation). Nothing at all wrong with that, just different from what we've put together.

These steps make up the core of the Ordo's Alchemical Practice, and the rituals that bring them about are the heart of the practice. Nothing here is truly hidden; simply do the work and you will develop eyes to see. In addition to the work, studying and then analyzing key Alchemical Texts give the Alchemist greater insight and a broader understanding of this particular tradition, which is one of Internal Hermetic Alchemy. The Internal Alchemy taught here is one in which we pair ingestion of Plant Elixirs created through Spagery and Astrological Magic with Internal Mineral Alchemy, in order to refine our Matter.

There are other Alchemical Traditions that practice Internal Refinement of the Metals which, in addition to using the sexual energies as we do through internal stimulation of the Center in which they are stored within our Earth, also consume the alchemically prepared sexual substances of the male and female (in addition to the female menstruate) as part of the refinement. This is completely valid, and is also the practice of some of our Indian Tantric-Alchemical Brothers who are rumored to be either the source of, or a co-evolving tradition with that we have learned from the Egyptians of old. This method isn't delineated here, but an Alchemist who masters the Internal methods taught here will have no difficulty discerning the method for using these substances, which work quickly upon the matter, although not as gently as do ours.

Study the Alchemical definitions above so that when reading the Alchemical writings you might see with the correct eyes for interpreting Hermetic Internal Alchemy from the perspective of the Ordo.

METHOD:
THE RITUAL, STRUCTURE, AND PRACTICE

ORDO OCTOPI NIGRI PULVERI

IN OUR SMALL ORDO WE HAVE A REGULAR PRACTICE THAT, IN TIME AND if followed religiously and paired with study and understanding of classical alchemical emblems and texts, will result in accomplishment of the Alchemical goal. The alchemical Rituals are divided by nature below, and are conducted as written. Some of the Alchemical Processes are descriptions of observed changes in the First Matter resulting from practices and rituals, and therefore don't require a separate ritual practice to enact. It all comes down to **Calcination** in this system. Our method comes down to simply purifying the Vessel, Calcining the Prima Materia and the Metals directly, and coagulating the refined Virtue. We dissolve ourselves regularly into the sea of Mercury, the *mer de noms*, and descend into the blackness of putrefaction so that we may arise renewed.

I. PURIFICATION RITUALS

Ablution with Holy Water. The Banishing of Uninvited Spirits. The Tower of Art Ritual.

II. CALCINATION RITUALS

The Holy Yeheshua Rite. The Antimaquis Rite.

III. SUBLIMATION

This is a Result, the separation of the Volatile Inner Fires from the metals, and of the volatile spiritual nature from the physical. This is where we separate the fixed from the flying, and is the result of the Calcination of the First Matter and of the metals (the seven interior metals and their nature is explained later in this manuscript).

IV. Coagulation

The sublimation-coagulation states are a circulation of the subtle and volatile Spirit (in all of its expressions within the Alchemist... as his own Spirit, as the Inner Fire held in the nerve-centers that are the interior Metals) within the Vessel of the Sphere of Sensation. The Coagulation state occurs when the subtle essences that have been made to "fly" from the First Matter by the gentle heat of Calcination permeate the earthly First Matter, gradually refining the whole. Here the Toad is Chained to the Eagle, and the Fixed is married to the flying.

V. Dissolution Rituals

Meditation, the Death Litany of Saturn. This process is silently beholding existence – not active meditation involving Calcinations, but contemplation of the Azoth, which requires disciplining the mind. The Alchemist first destroys everything outside of himself, and then inside of himself, using the Death Litany of Saturn. This leads into the state of putrefaction, which is readily attained once the Saturnian force has risen.

VI Putrefaction

This is achieved through use of the Death Litany of Saturn ritual (in order to achieve a strong rising of the Saturnian Inner Fire), followed by regular Calcination and Dissolution practice. The Death Litany itself may be used as part of regular practice to promote dissolution, and is included in the ritual battery.

VII Incineration

This is accomplished with prayer.

VIII Multiplication

This is the work of nature, and is accomplished with prayer.

RITES AND RITUAL COMPONENTS

Ritual organization: Our Golden Dawn Heritage

The organization of our ritual work is rooted in the Alchemical organization of ritual in the Golden Dawn and RR et AC. The Golden Dawn is fundamentally an Alchemical order; the purifications and calcinations are at first done analogically through Ritual Magic, and then directly through Alchemical work that is similar to the calcinations we use in our Ordo. Ritual magic alone is a Lunar, analogical Magic, and works upon the metals through manipulation of Symbol. Alchemical magic is Solar and Direct magic; it works directly upon the Metals and Cinnabar Fields within the body. Lunar magic is gentle in its effect, but is also slower acting. A comparatively low heat is placed upon the matter. Our work is a combination of the two, and the heat placed upon the matter can be intense.

Interestingly, not all Golden Dawn orders these days have an understanding of their own Alchemical heritage. The Hermetic Order of the Golden Dawn/Alpha et Omega is one that has full Alchemical contacts and understanding; this is the Order in which I've had my education. The techniques of this Order have their roots and foundations in the Hermetic tradition and the alchemical Golden Dawn.

THE KAMEA

The Sigils of the entities worked with in our system of Alchemical development are drawn from the Kamea, which are Magic Squares (as given us by Agrippa) that are symbolic of the Planets. As symbols, they have power to connect with the Macrocosmic force they represent. The Kamea themselves are arrangements of numbers that, when added vertically and diagonally, give the same sum. Drawn with Flashing Colors (the color appropriate for the Planet and its complimentary color) the Kamea become powerful talismans. They aren't necessary to all of our core rituals, but they are an important tool for working with the Metals using lunar Ceremonial magic.

On the *Picatrix*

The *Picatrix* is a book of Arabic Astrological magic that served as a major source for Heinrich Cornelius Agrippa, the renaissance era Magician whose work *Three Books Of Occult Philosophy* is a primary source for the Western Mystery Tradition. The *Picatrix* gives us the names of the Planetary spirits of the Directions that we use in our Antimaquis rite. Christopher Warnock (my instructor in Astrological Magic) and John Michael Greer published a full translation of the *Picatrix* in English that serves as source material for us. Christopher Warnock teaches an excellent course on astrological magic, which I've found invaluable in my own practice. The *Picatrix* we use is available at www.renaissanceastrology.com

The Altar Setup

The altar should be a simple table that can be covered with a white cloth. Upon the altar should be the Elemental Candles, arranged Fire, Water, Spirit, Air, Earth, from right to left. There should be your bowl of Holy Water. The Kamea of the Planet being worked that day should also be upon the altar, with incense for the planet and a candle. The incense should be lit once the Antimaquis rite has begun. The candle and incense for the Planet are placed atop the Kamea. An image of the Planetary God and of Azoth are useful and good to have, but are not completely necessary.

The Sign of the Enterer

As taken from the Golden Dawn Z3 document, and used in this system because its founder was trained in the Golden Dawn in the art of ceremonial Magic, because it just plain works. We do not use the Assumption of the Godform during the Sign of the Enterer (although it is certainly practiced during the restorative Spagyric alchemical practices of the Book of the Blossoming Flower). This is a key component in Golden Dawn Magic, but I have found it to be unnecessary for the aspect of the Sign we use, which is projection of LVX.

Standing as before described, in the form of the God, and elevating the mind to the contemplation of Kether, take the step like a stroke with the foot, bring the

arms above the head as if touching the Kether, and as the step is completed bring the arms over the head forwards. Thrust them out directly from the eyes horizontally – arms extended, fingers straight, palms downwards, the hands directed towards the object it is wished to charge or to affect. At the same time, sink the head till the eyes look exactly between the thumbs. In this way, the rays from the eyes, from each finger and from the thumbs, must all converge upon the object attacked. If any of them disperse, it is a weakness.

Thus performed, this Sign is a symbol of tremendous attacking force and of projection of will power, and it should be employed in all cases where force of attack is required – especially in charging of Talismans and the like. Generally, it is best to have the thumbs and all the fingers extended – but if a particular effect is desired, you may extend only the fingers appropriate thereto, keeping the rest folded back in the hand. Herewith also, may be combined the attribution of the Planets to the head (as explained in the Microcosm lecture), sending at the same time as imaginary ray of color of the Planet desired from the part of the head attributed to it. But, when finished, be careful to withdraw the rays again or they will remain like so many outlets of astral force and thus exhaust you. The best way to protect yourself against this is to give the Sign of Silence immediately. For the first Sign should always be answered by the second. The secret names of the Saluting Sign is "The Attacking Sign" or "The Sign of the Enterer of the Threshold."

We perform this Sign with another alteration. We step forward with the left foot, and, moving the body first, thrust the Arms out slowly with Hands extended so that the Palm of the hand is extended toward the object, and not the fingertips. The fingertips are reserved for Mudra-based work in which the individual fingers project LVX related to their Elemental/Planetary/Astrological attribution, and the gates within the palms work extremely well for projection/inhalation of LVX.

THE SIGN OF SILENCE

As taken from the Golden Dawn Z3 document, and used in this system because its founder was trained in the Golden Dawn in the art of ceremonial Magic. We do use the Godform of HARPOCRATES for this; it is impossible to do otherwise, for the sign itself is also his form. This isn't done in our understanding to recall a force, so much as to seal it where it has been sent.

The Sign of Silence withdraws the force put out by the Sign of the Enterer. Take upon thyself as before taught the colossal form of the God Harpocrates. Bring the left foot sharply back, both heels together – beat the ground once with the left foot as it is placed besides the right. Bring the left hand to the mouth and touch the lower lip with the left fore-finger. Close the other fingers and thumb, and drop the right hand to the side. Imagine that a watery vapor encircles and encloses you. This is the reflux of the current.

This Sign is also used as a protection against attack. The Sign represents a concentration of astral light about the person. Having given the Sign as above, it is a protection against all attack and danger of obsession. To make it stronger, the form of the God should be taken. If Spiritual force is required, formulate as if standing on a Lotus or rising from it. For force in contemplation and meditation, formulate as if seated upon a Lotus. But for more material force, as if standing upon a Dragon or a Serpent like some statues of Harpocrates. As a defense and protection, the Sign is as strong as the banishing pentagram, though of a different nature. And as the Sign of the Enterer represents attack, so does this sign represent defense thereto, as a shield is a defense against the Sword. From this Sign is a formula of invisibility derived.

The Secret Names of this Sign are: "The Sign of the God of Silence" or the "Sign of Defense or Protection." It may be performed with any finger of either hand, but it is most protective when the left forefinger is used, the Water of Chesed, for the fingers of the right hand represent more violent action, and those of the left more watery action.

It may here be remarked that the so-called Christian Sign of Benediction, consisting of the thumb and first two fingers only, projected, is the affirmation of Osiris, Isis and Nephthys – or Spirit, Fire, and Water.

With regard to taking on mentally the forms of the Gods, it may here be noted that the process is of great assistance and use in all magical working, whether of invocation or of evocation, contemplation, meditation, skrying in the spirit vision, alchemy, etc. For the forms of the Gods do here represent a certain symbolic material action of the Divine Forces.

THE BELLOWS BREATH

The Bellows Breath is a deep, slow and powerful breathing technique that, paired with the focused awareness of the Alchemist, concentrates and intensifies the LVX in a given area. It is the Four-Fold Breath of the Golden Dawn, it is the Pranayama one sees in Indian Yoga. The inhalation and exhalation of breath in the Alchemist is as the inhalation and exhalation of breath in God; it is the most powerful tool we have for refinement and development, for in breathing we imitate God as he creates and extinguishes existence.

To perform the Bellows Breath, we place the mental awareness at the part/object we wish to "cook" – to fill with the un-natural heat of the LVX. We gently "hold" it with our mind, wrapping our awareness about it. Then, we take deep and slow breaths, intensifying the action of the LVX present, which will quickly become agitated and seek to volatize with just the attention of our Mind. Where the Mind goes, the LVX follows.

MOVING THE AWARENESS

(Creating the Vortex of LVX within the body and within the Metals in order to aid in their Calcination.)

Moving the Awareness about the Body stimulates it, and as the LVX goes where the mind and concentration goes, moving the awareness about the Body is moving the LVX throughout the body. The point of Awareness is activated by concentrating on the thing you wish to stimulate, and feeling it. That point of feeling paired with concentration is the Awareness.

We use vortexes of LVX to stimulate the body's subtle component (which, as Mercury, interpenetrates the physical component); stirring the substance of the Metals and enlivening them. After Calcining a Metal – which is simply holding it in your awareness and performing the Bellows Breath – continue to hold it in your awareness, and move its substance in a clockwise motion. This being the direction the Sun moves, turning the Metals clockwise is turning them toward the Sun (Gold), and counter-clockwise away from the Sun (toward materiality, or Lead). The use of the Vortex can also be seen in the **Ouroboros**. The serpent biting its own tail is a symbol for a circular movement of LVX, from Earth to Heaven, back down to Earth and up to Heaven again.

This movement between Heaven and Earth is seen in the myth of Prometheus, and also in the Hermetic Axiom.

Within our alchemical Imagery the Vortex (which is also the Circumambulation of the Golden Dawn) is represented by the Ouroboros, whether that circulation is within an individual Metal or within the broader Vessel of the working Alchemist.

THE SOLAR-CROSS RITUAL

This is the Golden Dawn ritual of the Rose Cross, effective for sealing the Sphere of Sensation and shrouding it in Hermetic Silence, as given at www.hermetics.org.

1. Light a stick of incense. Go to the South East corner of the room. Make a large cross and circle thus:

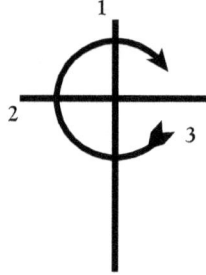

and holding the point of the incense in the center vibrate the word Yeheshuah.

2. With arm outstretched on a level with the center of the cross, and holding the incense stick, go to the South West corner and make a similar cross, repeating the Word.

3. Go to the North West corner and repeat the cross and the Word.

4. Go to the North East corner and repeat the cross and the Word.

5. Complete your circle by returning to the South East corner and bringing the point of the incense to the central point of the first cross which you should visualize there.

6. Holding the stick on high, go to the center of the room, walking diagonally across the room towards the North West corner. In the center of the room, above your head, trace the cross and circle and vibrate the Name.

7. Holding the stick on high, go to the North West and bring the point of the stick down to the center of the astral cross there.

8. Turn towards the South East and retrace your steps there, but now, holding the incense stick directed across the floor. In the center of the room, make the cross and circle towards the floor, as it were, under your feet, and vibrate the Name.

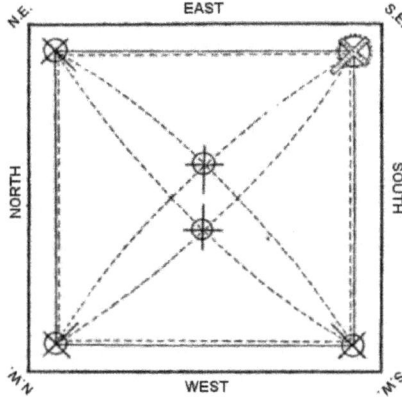

9. Complete this circle by returning to the South East and bringing the point of the stick again to the center of the Cross, then move with arm outstretched to S.W. corner.

10. From the center of this cross, and, raising stick before, walk diagonally across the room towards the North East corner. In the center of the room, pick up again the cross above your head previously made, vibrating the Name. It is not necessary to make another cross.

11. Bring the stick to the center of the North East cross and return to the South West, incense stick down, and pausing in the center of the room to link up with the cross under your feet.

12. Return to the South West and rest the point of the incense a moment in the center of the cross there. Holding the stick out, retrace your circle to the North West, link on to the N.W. Cross – proceed to the N.E. cross and complete your circle by returning to the S.E., and the center of the first cross.

13. Retrace the cross, but larger, and make a big circle, vibrating for the lower half Yeheshuah, and for the upper half Yehovashah.

Return to the center of the room, and end your ritual with gratitude and a clap of the hands.

PURIFICATION RITUALS

The Ablution with Holy Water

To make water Holy, first insert a few leaves of cleansing Hyssop, which has cleansing as one of its properties. Placing your hands over the bowl, Incant "In the name of **YEHESHUAH**, may this water be pure and Holy." Draw an equal-armed cross within a circle of white-golden light inside the water. And it is Holy.

The equal-armed Cross is a symbol of the union of Heaven and Earth. The circle around the cross adds to the symbolism, referring to union of Heaven and Earth within the boundaries of the World/Existence.

Using the right hand, draw an equal-armed Cross inside the holy water, and then surround it with a circle. Now you have Holy Water.

The Ablution itself is a simple spiritual bath. Take up the bowl of Holy Water, and dip the fingers of your right hand into it. Flick the Holy Water over your head three times and intone "AZOTH, root and Source of Being, wash away my iniquities. Cleanse me of all my impurity." Wash the Head, Genitals and Heart with the Holy water. Pour this water immediately outside of your home, or outside of a window. Avoid pouring it down drains, as this allows the unclean Spirit to remain in your home.

The Banishing of Uninvited Spirits

Light the charcoal within the censor. Breathe upon it seven times. Take up a pinch of banishing powder (made with equal parts burdock root and acacia leaves, ground as finely as possible; a grainy texture is fine) and burn it within the censor. The Burdock root is offensive to unclean spirits, and the Acacia leaves are encouraging to positive ones. As the smoke rises, vibrate strongly internally and externally "HEKAS HEKAS EST BEBELOI!" (This is an old banishing formula used in the Western Grimoire-Magic tradition.) Cense the corners of the room (including yourself), and it is cleansed.

THE ANGELIC SUMMONING RITE

Creating the Tower of Art

This rite uses **Come Here, Angel** Powder. (It can certainly be accomplished without it, but this layer of materia is important and should be included if possible.) This powder uses the virtue inherent in the materia to encourage the Angelic forces to attend, as the powder contains elements pleasing to the natures of the individual Angelic forces involved. The powder also acts as a "sacrifice" to the Angelic entities. Using the powder along with the vibratory incantation, visualization, and movement allows us to make an offering to the forces simultaneously with the summoning.

Come Here, Angel Powder
Ingredients:

Angelica Root, Dried Rose Petal, Red Pepper, Ginger Powder, Sugar, and Sea Salt.

Angelica Root to generally attract the forces.
Dried Rose petal is pleasing to Air entities.
Red Pepper is pleasing to Fire entities.
Ginger Powder is pleasing to Water entities.
Sea Salt (as a crystal) is pleasing to Earth entities.
Sugar is there to sweeten them toward you and towards your Work.

Grind the ingredients together using a Mortar and Pestle, moving clockwise. Lean close to the Mortar and Inhale the scent of the mixture. Upon exhale, vibrate "AMEN" and use your awareness and Breath to project white-golden LVX into the mixture (Perform the Sign of the Enterer). Perform the Sign of Silence, and visualize the powder surrounded in a blue mist, in order to seal the current of virtue (LVX) within the powder.

Take up a pinch of the **Come Here, Angel** powder and place it upon the burning coal in the censor. Facing the East, draw an Invoking Air Pentagram whilst vibrating **"Yod He Vau He"**. See it as a rich golden yellow. In a vibrant and royal purple, draw and vibrate the Hebrew letters that spell the Archangel's name **"RAFAEL"** within the Pentagram. Project LVX into the Pentagram.

רפאל

State powerfully and respectfully, "Come here, great Archangel RAFAEL, and stand in the East with me before God".

Take up another Pinch of the summoning powder. Turning clockwise to the south, and vibrate powerfully **"ADONAI"** whilst drawing an invoking Fire pentagram in brilliant red. In a rich and bright green, draw and vibrate the Hebrew letters that spell the Archangel's name **"MICHAEL"** within the pentagram. Perform the Sign of the Enterer.

מכאל

State powerfully and respectfully, "Come here, great Archangel **MICHAEL**, and stand in the South with me before God."

Add another pinch of the summoning powder to the burning censer. Facing the East (moving ever clockwise), draw an Invoking Water

Pentagram in deep blue whilst vibrating "**EHIEH**". In a bright and fiery orange, draw and vibrate the Hebrew letters that spell the Archangel's name "**GABRIEL**" within the Pentagram. Perform the Sign of the Enterer.

גבריאל

State powerfully and respectfully, "Come here, great Archangel **GABRIEL**, and stand in the West with me Before God."

Add another pinch of the summoning powder to the censer, and turn to the North. Draw an Invoking Earth Pentagram in throbbing black whilst vibrating "**AGLA**". In a glowing and blinding white, draw and vibrate the Hebrew letters and name of the Archangel "**URIEL**". Perform the Sign of the Enterer.

אוריאל

State Powerfully and Respectfully, "Come here, great Archangel **URIEL**, and stand in the North with me Before God."

Sometimes the Angels will make their presence known visually, usually through sensation. A change in atmosphere, a smell, a sound. If you perform the invocation correctly, they Will attend.

Turn and face the East. Add a final pinch of the summoning powder. Before you and somewhat above you, draw a Hexagram (moving clockwise) in rich golden light, vibrating the Holy Name of the Sun "**YHVH ELOA VE DAATH**". Within the Hexagram, in a blinding white light, draw the letters of your Daimon's name. If you have yet to discover its name, draw **AZOTH**.

State powerfully and respectfully, "Come here, Holy Daimon "N.", and Stand within me in Adoration before God".

Visualize and feel a thick beam of almost physical and electric white light descending from above and encompassing your sphere. In the center of this light, from your Heart, perceive the form and feeling of your Daimon blossoming to life within your sphere.

This ritual is a preparatory ritual, done to prepare the Alchemical Vessel - the Sphere of Sensation - for the work of Calcination that follows. The Tower of Art is the cleansed, balanced and pure Sphere of Sensation. It is a stable place from which the Alchemist can do his work. A clean vessel is important, as we wouldn't want any dross tainting our work with the First Matter.

CALCINATION, SUBLIMATION, AND COAGULATION RITUALS

THE HOLY YEHESHUA RITE

This rite is based on a combination of techniques that are central to modern Western Magic, but which are seldom used with one another. It involves Invocation of a Godform, Bardonian Mantra and pore breathing, Golden Dawn-style vibration and Hoodoo-style Materia/Candle Magic. (It can be performed without the Materia if necessary, if for instance one is on a train and not in Temple, but it is much better to include the Elemental Candles.) This rite is used to bring elementally-tuned LVX, which is the Alchemical Un-Natural Fire, into the vessel in balanced amounts. It is also meant, through the power of Lunar/Analogical magic, to balance the Elements of the personality of the Alchemist, and also the elements of the body. The LVX is then set to Sublimate and gently calcine the First Matter. This is much "gentler" than working directly on the Metals, but accomplishes the same thing... just over a much longer period of time. At the end of the rite, we incant the holy name "YEHESHUA" whilst breathing out, and moving the awareness down the body and Sphere of Sensation (where the Awareness goes, the LVX follows), as this is symbolic of the Heavens descending into the Earth. We then move the awareness upward while vibrating "YEHOVASHA", which is symbolic of Earth ascending into Heaven. This circulation and rite contains the essence of Alchemical practice, which relies upon gentle application of Heat and the Sublimation and Circulation of Spirit, which is LVX in motion. We are using the gentle Un-natural fire to heat the furnace of the Body; this furnace in turn gently heats the Vessel, and that which is contained within the Vessel is gently calcined and refined, and soon through the process of Sublimation the metals release their Vapor, Separating the subtle from the gross and the fixed from the volatile, which is circulated and then Coagulates, sinking deep into our nature and altering that nature. This marries the fixed to the volatile flying, re-invigorating the body that is our First Matter. The further steps of Dissolution and Putrefaction have separate rites; the First Matter will go through these stages if there is continued Calcination. The stages of Incineration and Multiplication are entirely the work of Nature, and require nothing but continued Calcination and prayer from the Alchemist.

We have rituals that work directly upon the metals, so as to assist Nature in her process. The Holy Yeheshuah Rite alone heats very gently and generally. We apply intense direct heat with the Antimaquis Rite, and encourage the Planetary Metals within the body to release their Vapor and, with the aid of Mercury, become Gold.

As an aid to invocation of and development with the Elemental forces, dressed and consecrated candles are used in combination with the other techniques of this rite. They are not difficult to make, and once made can be used by simply lighting them. Each candle is dressed with an oil and certain Herbs that are known to carry the virtue of the Element it is to express. I think of them as elemental Engines; they are used to augment the natural reserves of each element the Magician has, and to fill the atmosphere of the temple (both the Body and the external temple) with their influence. Each candle should be dressed in a Planetary oil that corresponds to the ruler of its Astrological Triplicity, as designated by William Lilly in *Christian Astrology*, 1604.

◊ Earth is ruled by Venus
◊ Water is ruled by Mars
◊ Air is ruled by Mercury and Saturn
◊ Fire is ruled by Jupiter and the Sun

To make Oils, simply follow the instructions within the Book of the Blossoming Flower, appended to this manuscript.

Dress the Earth candle with Oil of Venus, and with the Herbs that contain the virtue of the Planet Venus; Jasmine, Cherry, and Datura serve well. All will serve well, just be sure to include at least one herb from each of the planetary rulers.

Dress the Water candle with Oil of Mars, and with herbs that contain the virtue of the Planet Mars; Ginger, Acacia, and Basil serve well. All will serve well, just be sure to include at least one herb from each of the planetary rulers.

Dress the Air candle in Oil of Mercury and Saturn, and with herbs that correspond to both planets; Poppy, Celery, and Fennel are Mercurial; Mandrake, Nightshade, Cannabis and Solomon's Seal are Saturnian. All will serve well, just be sure to include at least one herb from each of the planetary rulers.

Dress the Fire candle in Oil of Jupiter and Oil of Sol, and with herbs that correspond to and contain the virtue of both Planets: Anise, Mint, and Nutmeg are Jupiterian; Chamomile, Hibiscus, and Sunflower are Solar. All will serve well, as long as one herb from each of the planetary rulers is included.

Dress the Spirit candle in Holy oil, made using Burdock and Angelica root. Dried rose petals are the only herb necessary for dressing.

Before Dressing the Candle, carve the Alchemical symbol of the Element. They are as follows:

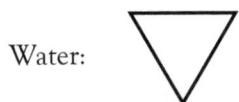

Earth:

Fire:

Air:

Water:

Spirit:

After dressing the candle with these substances pray over each with the Elemental Prayer as given to us by Eliphas Levi in *Transcendental Magic*, 1850, and then project LVX using the Sign of the Enterer into the candle itself. The LVX should be the color of the Elemental Candle; the Alchemist inhales and draws in LVX visualized as the Element's color, and then exhales and projects. Seal the volatile virtue within the candle, "fixing it", using the Sign of Silence, visualizing that the blue mist surrounds the candle and prevents the Virtue from seeping away. The Elemental prayers are as follows:

THE PRAYER OF THE GNOMES (EARTH)

Invisible King who has taken the earth as a support, and who has dug abysses in order to fill them with the omnipotence! Thou whose name makest the arches of the world tremble! Thou who makest the seven metals circulate in the veins of stone; Monarch of seven luminaries Rewarder of subterranean workmen! bring us to the desirable air and to the kingdom of light. We watch and work without respite. We seek and hope by the twelve stones of the Holy City, for the talismans which are buried by the magnetic nail which passes through the center of the earth. Lord! Lord! Lord! Have pity upon those who suffer! Enlarge our hearts! Let us be free and raise up our heads! Exalt us! O stability and movement! O Day invested by night! O Darkness veiled in light! O Master who never retainest the wages of thy workmen! O silvery whiteness! O Golden Splendor! O Crown of Diamonds, living and melodious! Thou who bearest the sky upon thy finger, like a ring of sapphire! Thou who hidest under the earth, in the kingdom of gems, the wonderful seed of stars! All hail! Reign; and be the Eternal Dispenser of riches, of which thou hast made us the guardians. Amen.

THE PRAYER OF THE UNDINES (WATER)

Terrible king of the sea! Thou who boldest the keys of the cataracts of heaven, and who enclosest the subterranean waters in the hollow places of the earth! King of the deluge and of rains, of springtime! Thou who openest the sources of streams and fountains! Thou who commandest the moisture(which is like the blood of the earth) to become the sap of plants! We adore and invoke thee! Speak to us, ye moving and changeable creatures! Speak to us in the great commotions of the sea, and we will tremble before thee. Speak to us also in the murmur of the limpid waters, and we will desire thy love. O immensity in which all the rivers of being lose themselves, which ever spring up anew in us! O ocean of infinite perfections! Height which beholdeth thee in the depth! Depth which breathes thee forth in the height! Bring us to the true life through intelligence and love! Lead us to immortality through sacrifice, in order that one day we may be found worthy to offer thee water, blood, and tears, for the remission of sins. Amen.

THE PRAYER OF THE SYLPHS (AIR)

Spirit of light! Spirit of wisdom! whose breath gives and takes away again the forms of all things! Thou, in whose presence the life of being is a shadow which changes, and a vapor which passes away. Thou who ascendest the clouds and movest on the wing of the winds. When thou breathes! forth, infinite spaces are peopled! When thou inhalest, all that comes from thee returns to thee! Endless movement in eternal stability, be thou eternally blest! We praise thee and bless thee in the changing empire of created light, of shadows, of reflections and of images; and we long unceasingly for thine immutable and imperishable light. Let the ray of thy intelligence and the heat of thy love penetrate even to us; then what is movable will become fixed; the shadow will become a body; the spirit of the air will become a soul; the dream will become a thought, and we shall no longer be borne away by the tempest, but shall hold the bridle of the winged steeds of the morning, and shall direct the course of the evening winds that we may fly into thy presence. O spirit of spirits! O eternal soul of souls! O imperishable breath of life! O creative inspiration. O mouth which inspires and respires the existence of all beings in the flux and reflux of thy eternal Word, which is the divine ocean of movement and of truth. Amen!

The Prayer of the Salamanders (FIRE)

Immortal, eternal, ineffable and uncreated Father of all things I who are borne upon the incessantly rolling chariot of Worlds which are always turning; Ruler of the ethereal immensity where the throne of thy power is elevated; from whose height thy dread-inspiring eyes discover all things, and thy exquisite and sacred ears hear all; Listen to thy children whom thou hast loved from the beginning of the ages; for thy golden, great, and eternal majesty is resplendent above the world and the starry heavens. Thou art raised above them O sparkling fire! There thou dost illumine and support thyself by thine own splendor; and there comes forth from thine essence overflowing streams of light which nourish thine infinite spirit. That infinite spirit nourishes all things, and renders this inexhaustible treasure of substance always ready for the generation which fashions it and which receives in itself the forms with which thou hast impregnated it from the beginning. From this spirit those most holy kings who surround thy throne, and who compose thy court, derive their origin. O Father Universal! Only One! O Father of blessed mortals and immortals! Thou hast specially created powers who are marvelously like thine eternal thought and adorable essence. Thou hast established them superior to the angels who announce to the world thy wishes. Finally thou hast created us in the third rank in our elementary empire. There our continual employment is to praise thee and adore thy wishes. There we incessantly burn with the desire of possessing thee, O Father! O Mother! the most tender of all mothers! O admirable archetype of maternity and pure love! O Son, the flower of sons! O Form of all forms; soul, spirit, harmony and number of all things. Amen.

The Candle of Spirit is created using the Lord's Prayer, which should be understood esoterically as an invocation of the Holy Guardian Angel. Read this prayer, with a true understanding of what Heaven and the Kingdom refer to, and you will see.

Our Father
Who art in Heaven
Hallowed be thy name
Thy Kingdom come
Thy Will be done
On Earth as it is in Heaven
Give us this day our daily bread
And forgive us our trespasses
As we forgive those who trespass against us
And lead us not into temptation
But deliver us from evil
For thine is the Kingdom
The power
And the glory
Forever and ever.
Not my will, but thine be done.

Making the Elemental candles is straightforward and simple, and they add depth and atmosphere to our ritual work in addition to being a simple way to evoke the elements.

The candles should be arranged on the altar, from Right to Left: Fire, Water, Spirit, Air, Earth.

MUDRA

For each of the Elements invoked and breathed during the Holy Yeheshuah Rite there is a Mudra; using this Mudra in combination with pore breathing and incantation allows for immediate and deep connection and access to the elemental Virtues. There are many practical uses for this beyond Theurgic development. Elemental entities may be summoned and communicated with, rooms may be impregnated and made suitable for purposes related to one element or the other, talismans and amulets charged, ailments treated... the only real limit to its use is in the understanding of the Adept using it.

THE FIRE MUDRA

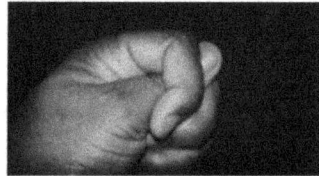

THE WATER MUDRA

THE AIR MUDRA

THE EARTH MUDRA

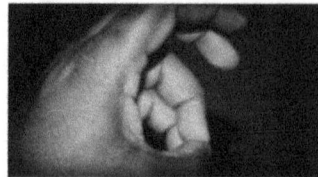

THE SPIRIT MUDRA

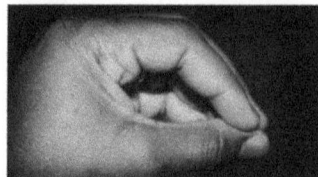

During the Holy Yeheshuah Rite, the Mudra is used at the same time that the Letter of Power is vibrated into existence within the Sphere of the Alchemist. This accomplishes a number of things. By intently visualizing and feeling the Elemental power come into being during the rite, we are training the LVX, the sea of Mind, the Azoth, to answer that specific action with a concentration of the particular Elemental power in our sphere or environment. After this has been done long enough, the Mudra alone is enough to invoke the force, and the vibration and visualization will further reinforce the Mudra in addition to strengthening the general invocation of the force. So, each time this is used, the rite becomes more effective and the Mudra becomes more effective.

RITUAL SUMMARY

1. Perform the Qabalistic Cross if you have not already done so.

2. Light the Fire Candle, Perform the Fire Mudra, and Summon Fire, vibrating YOD deeply. Pore Breath into your body and Sphere 5 times, filling yourself with fiery LVX.

3. Light the Water Candle, Perform the Water Mudra and Summon Water, vibrating HEH deeply. Pore Breath into your body and Sphere 5 times.

4. Light the Air Candle, Perform the Air Mudra and Summon Air, vibrating VAU deeply. Pore Breath into your body and Sphere 5 times.

5. Light the Earth Candle, Perform the Earth Mudra and Summon Earth, vibrating HEH deeply. Pore Breath into your body and Sphere 5 times.

6. Light the Spirit Candle, Perform the Spirit Mudra and Summon Spirit, vibrating SHIN deeply. Pore Breath into your body and Sphere 5 times.

7. Vibrate the Holy Name "YEHESHUAH" six times (minimum), and Vibrate the Holy Name "YEHOVASHA" six times (minimum), rotating front to back and side to side, creating an Ouroboros of LVX within your Sphere of Sensation, and perform the Sign of Silence.

THE QABALISTIC CROSS

Stand facing the East. Close your eyes, and visualize yourself growing large in Spirit, till you stand with the Earth at your feet, and Stars swirling about you. Above you is a brilliant, near-blinding white light. Raise your wand above your head and touch this Sea of Light. Draw the light down into your Heart and Vibrate:

"ATEH"

Bring the wand down until it points at your sexual organs/centers and, visualizing a brilliant light shooting up from the Earth at your feet to meet the light now in your heart, forming a pillar of light, Vibrate:

"MALKUTH"

Bring the tip of the wand to your right shoulder, touching it lightly. Visualize a ray of light entering your body from the right and meeting the pillar at your heart. This ray should begin further away than can be perceived, and end in the heart. Vibrate as you touch:

"VE-GEBURAH"

Take the wand across the body, and touch the left shoulder. Visualize a ray piercing through the left side and entering the heart, whilst vibrating:

"VE-GEDULAH"

Take up the Wand and move it in a clockwise circle over the heart, vibrating:

"LE-OLAM"

Raise the wand in a sign of respect, and vibrate:

"AMEN"

Take three deep, slow breaths, and then return to the body.

Use the Qabalistic Cross in the beginning of your ritual batteries to center yourself. The God-Names can awaken and invigorate the energetic bodies, and build structures within upon which we will hang the entire Tree of Life, over time.

Light the FIRE Candle.

Create the Fire Mudra, and Vibrate the Hebrew letter "YOD". Visualize before you (but within the confines of your Sphere of Sensation) the letter in a bright and vibrant Red, outlined in its flashing color Green.

Inhale deeply, and as you do, draw in the LVX-Fire through the Yod into your Sphere of Sensation and Body. See your Sphere of Sensation as Red in Harmony with the essence of YOD. Inhale into yourself again (using the Pore Breathing technique) and upon exhale, Vibrate YOD again while surrounding your body with your awareness. Repeat the inhalation and vibration of YOD five times. While you vibrate YOD, become aware of the heat and vitality of your body. Inhale and release the Mudra. Upon exhale, breathe the Red out of your Aura so that it is clear in your vision.

Light the WATER Candle.

Now create the Water Mudra, and Vibrate the Hebrew letter "HEH". Visualize before you (but within the confines of your Sphere of Sensation) the letter in a bright and vibrant Blue, outlined in its flashing color Orange.

Inhale deeply, and as you do, draw in the LVX-Water through the HEH into your Sphere of Sensation and Body. See your Sphere of Sensation as Blue in Harmony with the essence of HEH. Inhale into yourself again (using the Pore Breathing technique) and upon exhale, Vibrate HEH again while surrounding your body with your awareness. Repeat the inhalation and vibration of HEH five times. Inhale and release the Mudra. Upon exhale, breathe the Blue out of your Aura so that it is clear in your vision.

Light the AIR candle.

Next, create the Air Mudra, and Vibrate the Hebrew letter "VAU". Visualize before you (but within the confines of your Sphere of Sensation) the letter in a bright and vibrant Yellow, outlined in its flashing color Purple.

Inhale deeply, and as you do, draw in the LVX-Air through the VAU into your Sphere of Sensation and Body. See your Sphere of Sensation as Yellow in Harmony with the essence of VAU. Inhale into yourself again (using the Pore Breathing technique) and upon exhale, Vibrate VAU again while surrounding your body with your awareness. Repeat the inhalation and vibration of VAU five times. Inhale and release the Mudra. Upon exhale, breathe the Yellow out of your Aura so that it is clear in your vision.

Light the EARTH candle.

Create the Earth Mudra, and Vibrate the Hebrew letter "HEH". Visualize before you (but within the confines of your Sphere of Sensation) the letter in a dark and vibrant Black, outlined in its flashing color White.

Inhale deeply, and as you do, draw in the LVX-Earth through the HEH into your Sphere of Sensation and Body. See your Sphere of Sensation as Black in Harmony with the essence of HEH. Inhale into yourself again (using the Pore Breathing technique) and upon exhale, Vibrate HEH again while surrounding your body with your awareness. Repeat the inhalation and vibration of HEH five times. Inhale and release the Mudra. Upon exhale, breathe the Black out of your Aura so that it is clear in your vision.

Light the SPIRIT candle.

Create the Spirit Mudra, and Vibrate the Hebrew letter "SHIN". Visualize before you (but within the confines of your Sphere of Sensation) the letter in a bright and vibrant White.

Inhale deeply, and as you do, draw in the LVX-Spirit through the SHIN into your Sphere of Sensation and Body. See your Sphere of Sensation as White, in Harmony with the essence of SHIN. Inhale into yourself again (this time, visualize a shaft of white light descending from above, through your Crown, and enlightening your entire form) and upon exhale, Vibrate SHIN again while surrounding your body with your awareness. Repeat the inhalation and vibration of SHIN five times. Inhale and release the Mudra. Upon exhale, breathe the White out of your Aura so that it is clear in your vision.

Place your awareness within your central Cinnabar Field, at the Heart. Vibrate deeply and strongly the Holy Name "YEHESHUAH

YEHOVASHA" while holding your awareness within your center, and be sure to vibrate the name as strongly as you can. Now, place your awareness above your head in your Sphere of Sensation, and exhale moving your awareness down the front of your body, vibrate "YEHESHUA". The LVX descends from Heaven. Move your awareness up the back of your body while inhaling, vibrating internally "YEHOVASHA". The LVX ascends from Earth. Do this a total of six times, first front and back, and the left to right, and End with "AMEN".

This formula is also a powerful one for manifestation (through understanding of the Letters as keys to the Four Worlds), and may be used to empower talismans, birth spiritual entities, and in the rite of the Living Incantation (taught in the Ordo Octopi Nigri Pulveri) create a being or result by vibrating the Formula weaved into a purpose-built incantation. This brings the desired thing through the layers of existence and into a material Basis.

The Lemnian Fire Rite

This is the rite that we use to stimulate the Internal Fires of the metal from the root out, as opposed to from the "flower" in. The metals are rooted within the Alchemical body in the Cinnabar Fields; these are the three pools of Life emanated by the Spirit-body. They are a deep crimson in color, and like Cinnabar (which contains Sulfur and Mercury within it, which alludes to the nature of the internal Cinnabar fields, which are composed of primarily Alchemical Sulfur and Mercury, with a small measure of Salt) burn with an internal fire of their own; they are the fires from which the metals draw their own virtue. They are located behind the Navel, behind the Heart, and deep within the Brain. They are large, and these "locations" are merely where they are perceived by the awareness; they aren't quite physical and so do not have literal locations within the physical body, only signposts toward their general location within the structure of the Spirit Body.

The Cinnabar Field located behind the Navel "feeds" the Saturnian and Martial Metals within the body; they have their roots in the Cinnabar Field and draw their Natural Fire from it. The Cinnabar Field behind the Heart feeds the Solar and the Jupiterian metals. The Cinnabar field within the head feeds the Venusian, Lunar, and Mercurial Metals.

With the Lemnian Fire Rite we aim to augment the stores of Natural Fire within the body with the un-natural (meaning non-native) external fire; we fill the Cinnabar Fields in an even manner, allowing them to grow full and to refine the Virtue within them. Each of these is filled with the Secret Fire, and currents of this fire can be felt to rise and burn as serpents within the body as the Alchemist works with them.

There are three levels of Heat we apply with this rite:

The First is 3 breaths for each Cinnabar Field. 3.
The Second is 9 breaths for each field. 3x3.
The Third is 27 breaths for each field. 3x3x3.

The ritual is structured around first sensitizing the spiritual body, (manipulating its essence using the awareness and the External Fire), then opening the Gates (the mouth of the Alchemical Vessel) located at the top of the head and at the soles of the hands and the feet, and then filling the Cinnabar fields with the external Fire. It is much easier to breath the external fire into the Vessel from these gates than generally through the Pores; likely because it is easier for the mind to hold these smaller areas in the awareness than the whole body.

"Lemnian" is an allusion to Lemnos, where the God of Fire Vulcan has his forge; hence, the physical body, with its many secret fires, is the Lemnian Earth. The Lemnian Fire Rite stokes the flames of the Lemnian Earth.

The Lemnian Fire Rite – using the Vulcanic Breath

Begin by using mudra and vibration, and the awareness, to form a ball of LVX above the head, as wide around as the shoulders. Use the Mudra for each Element, in addition to vibration of and visualization of the Hebrew letter, to create this Sphere of LVX from all four elements and spirit, forming the name YEHESHUA. One breath of each letter is enough. Grasp this sphere with the awareness. Inhale, and fill it with the Unnatural Fire; remember that where the Mind goes the LVX follows.

Take the sphere and, upon exhaling, move it down and through the Alchemical Vessel (including the Lemnian Earth) exiting from the bottom of the feet. Inhale and bring the Sphere back above the Head, exhale and send it down through the feet once more. Repeat the descent and ascent nine times. This has a sensitizing effect on the subtle bodies, stimulating them in preparation for the influx of the external Fire and the stimulation and rising of the Internal Fire. Allow the sphere to dissipate.

Now we hold the gates – the mouths of our Vessel – with our minds, and invigorate them with three inhalations of the external fire. Begin first with the feet, and inhale the external fire directly into them. You will generally perceive a tingling or throbbing when they are stimulated and fully "awake", depending upon your sensitivity; this same throbbing or tingling can be perceived in any properly stimulated part of the spiritual body upon which the mind is focused. Do the same for the palms of the hands, and for the top of the head, and for the mouth and lungs. Now our Vessel is ready to take in great quantities of the external fire.

Hold the gates of the alchemical vessel in your awareness; now inhale, and as you do so draw the LVX into your head through the gates. The LVX taken in from the gates at the feet should be drawn up the center of the legs to the base of the spine, then up through the spine, and into the head. The LVX taken in from the gates at the hands should be drawn up through the center of the arms, through the shoulders and then up through the neck and into the head. The LVX taken in from the head should be drawn from above straight into the head. This should all happen during the inhale; upon exhale we push the inhaled fire into the cinnabar fields. Fill each field with the same number of breaths, working the bellows, beginning with the one in the belly, and then the one in the area of the heart (perceive these as being Behind the Metals), and finally that cinnabar field in the head. As the Fields are filled with the LVX, the external fire, they are stimulated and their internal fire is awakened. This internal fire is a Serpent (as opposed to an Eagle, as the virtue of the Metals is) which rises into the head as a subtle virtue. The rising of the fires within the cinnabar fields is often accompanied by a sensation of heat, and a quivering of the flesh. Whereas the virtue of the Metals is often tingling and invigorating, the fiery Serpents within the cinnabar fields are hot and visceral.

After some time working with this rite, a natural Ouroboros is formed; the fiery Serpent rises from the lower field into the middle and then the upper field, and then descends back into the lower field, refining the spiritual body and metals as it goes.

Begin with 3 repetitions for each Cinnabar Field, and then 9 when comfortable, and finally 27. This should be a gradual ramping up of heat and intensity; as the fires rise there will be personal and spiritual effects that require careful attention from the Alchemist. We call these sorts of breath Vulcanic breaths, as they cause the natural Fire within the Lemnian Earth to rise with force.

SOME FURTHER NOTES ON THE ALCHEMICAL BODY

The alchemical body contains ten primary structures which we concern ourselves with; there are the Seven Planetary Metals and the Cinnabar fields. The Planetary Metals draw their primary substance from the three Cinnabar fields, which draw their sustenance from the Soul. So, first there is One, which then differentiates into Three, and then into Seven, and from thence into physicality. The alchemical body mirrors the structure of the Macrocosm primarily, if not perfectly.

There are points of influx and out-flux on the Body, from which Fire and Light may be internalized and externalized. These are the Gates of the body, found at the top of the head, the bottoms of the feet, and the palms of the hands. With practice the entire body becomes porous to the LVX, and the unnatural fire can be inhaled directly into the being, as if the alchemist is breathing light in through the pores. Within the metals are the Eagles, the hidden fire and virtue held within the metals that is released with their refinement and calcination.

THE BELLOWS

The Bellows is the Lungs/Abdomen – the External Fire is brought into the body through the Gates of Influx and out-flux. The gates are located in the palms of the hands, the soles of the feet, the crown of the head, and the primary gate which is the Mouth and Nose. In normal breathing the external fire is inhaled directly into the lungs in small increments with the breath, where it is absorbed by the blood and coagulates in the body's cells with the nutrients liberated by the digestion process. With the Vulcanic breath much greater amounts of the external fire are brought into play. Upon exhale, the fire is moved (by moving the awareness... where the attention goes, the LVX follows) from the bellows toward the Metal that we aim to refine or the Field we wish to stimulate. This technique is an example of why we are an amalgam way. We join the Dry external heat with the Wet internal heat in order to refine our Earth.

THE RED DRAGONS – THE CINNABAR FIELDS

These refer to the great energetic pools that feed the Metals. They are located in the head, around/behind the Mercury, Lunar, and Venusian metals, in the Chest behind the Jupiterian and Solar metals, and in the Pelvis behind the Saturnian and Martian metals. They are fed directly by the Bellows, which is stoked by the breath during the hour of that Planet. These pools of Fire are the fountains through which the inner realm of Spirit penetrate and coagulate into physicality. They aren't tuned to a particular planet, but instead are of a pure combination of the alchemical substances (Sulfur, Mercury, and Salt) in balanced proportions, ever turning.

THE ANTIMAQUIS RITE

CREATING THE PLANETARY SPHERE AND CALCINING THE INDIVIDUAL METALS

This rite should be performed during the Planetary Hour of the Planet being Invoked. It consists of the names of certain Angels of the Planets as found in the *Picatrix* being invoked in their position about the Planet – and about the Alchemist – so that they surround and empower the Sphere of the Alchemist. The Sphere of Sensation's measure of that Planet's force is brought into perfect balance, and the authority of the Angels over other entities of the Planetary realms is available for the Alchemist's use. The names are vibrated into existence in their allotted place, and the Sphere is tuned, in color and vibration, to the Force of the Planet. From here, Invocations, Evocations, and the enlivening of talismans and amulets can be accomplished from a place of balanced power. In our Alchemical practice, we place our awareness around the Metals within the body and use the Bellows-Breath to create intense heat directly upon the Metal. It can also be used to create Gates to the plane of the Planet being invoked, through which the Planet's influence may be concentrated in a given space.

Begin facing the East. Turn your attention to the Planetary Metal within and the Symbol/Image of the Planet. Light the Planetary Incense and Candle-Engine, if you have made one for the Planet you're working with. Expand your Awareness to include your entire Aura. Vibrate powerfully the Hebrew God-Name associated with the Planet being worked.

> Saturn: YEHOVAH ELOHIM
> Jupiter: EL
> Mars: ELOHIM GIBOR
> Sol: YEHOVAH ELOA VE-DA'ATH
> Venus: YEHOVA TZABAOTH
> Mercury: ELOHIM TZABAOTH
> Luna: SHADAI EL CHAI

Now place the awareness in the Internal Metal of the Planet, and vibrate the name of the coadunate spirit of that Planet, as given in the *Picatrix*. This spirit embraces and joins all of the Planet's Names and Powers, collectively and individually, as a whole. Place your awareness above your head and state "Above me, N." where N. is the name of the Spirit Above. Place your awareness below your feet, and state "Below me, N." where N. is the name of the Spirit Below. Place your awareness to the right of your body and state "At my right, N." where N. is the name of the Spirit at Right. Place your awareness to the left of your body and state "At my left, N." where N. is the name of the Spirit at Left. Place your awareness in front of you, and state "Before me, N." where N. is the name of the Spirit at Front. Place your awareness behind you and state "Behind me, N." where N. is the name of the Spirit at Rear. Now, expand your awareness to include your entire Sphere of Sensation. Vibrate the name of the energizing spirit, the Spirit of the Planet's Motion. All of the Spirit Names should be vibrated powerfully, and in the color that is natural to the Planet. Visualize your sphere as vibrating in harmony with the Color of the Planet, and intone the Planetary Incantation. This will attune you to the Planet – from here you are prepared to conduct Calcination upon the interior Planet, as well as any magical work involving the Planet; from simple honoring of the Planetary God, to Evocation of its Spirits, creating Talismans, Divinations... conducting this ritual before any of the above places the Alchemical Adept in a balanced position for the Work.

The Internal Metals are as follows:

Saturn/Lead: The area of the perineum, at the base of the torso between the rectum and genitalia.

Mars/Iron: The area of the genitalia and lower belly.

Jupiter/Tin: The area of the Solar Plexus.

Sol/Gold: The area of the Heart Ganglia.

Venus/Bronze: The area of the Lymph Nodes, in the Throat.

Luna/Silver: The area of the Pineal Gland, which is in the brain but may be accessed by placing the awareness between the eyes. The Metals are rooted within the body, but express themselves like flowers in the body, so that they project a bit beyond the physical at full bloom.

Mercury/Mercury: The area of the pituitary gland, which is in the brain but may be accessed by placing the awareness at the top of the head.

The Coadunate Spirits of the Planets are as follows:

Saturn: REDIMEZ
Jupiter: DEMEHUZ
Mars: DEHARAYUZ
Sun: BEYDELUZ
Venus: DEYDEZ
Luna: HARNUZ
Mercury: MERHUYEZ

The Spirits Above of the Planets are as follows:

Saturn: TOZ
Jupiter: DERMEZ
Mars: HEHEYDIZ
Sun: DEHYMEX
Venus: HEYLUZ

Luna: HEDIZ
Mercury: AMIREZ

The Spirits Below of the Planets are as follows:

Saturn: COREZ
Jupiter: MATIZ
Mars: HEYDEYUZ
Sun: EYDULEZ
Venus: CAHYLUZ
Mercury: HYTYZ
Luna: MARAYUZ

The Spirits at Right of the Planets are as follows:

Saturn: DEYTYZ
Jupiter: MAZ
Mars: MAHARAZ
Sun: DEHEYFUZ
Venus: DIRUEZ
Mercury: CEHUZ
Luna: MELETAZ

The Spirits at Left of the Planets are as follows:

Saturn: DERIUZ
Jupiter: DERIZ
Mars: ARDAUZ
Sun: AZUHAFEZ
Venus: ABLEYMEZ
Mercury: DERIZ
Luna: TIMEZ

The Spirits Before of the Planets are as Follows:

Saturn: TALYZ
Jupiter: TAMIZ
Mars: HONDEHOYUZ

Sun: MAHABEYUZ
Venus: TEYLUZ
Mercury: MAYLEZ
Luna: HUEYEZ

The Spirits Behind of the Planets are as Follows:

Saturn: DARUZ
Jupiter: FORUZ
Mars: MEHEYEDIZ
Sun: HADYZ
Venus: ARZUZ
Mercury: DEHEDYZ
Luna: MEYNELUZ

The Spirits of Motion of the Planets throughout the Heavens are as Follows:

Saturn: TAHAYTUC
Jupiter: DEHYDEZ
Mars: DEHYDEMEZ
Sun: LETAHAYMERIZ
Venus: DEHATARYZ
Mercury: MEHENDIZ
Luna: DAHANUZ

Performing this rite will lead to Sublimation, as the direct heat will accelerate Nature's hand, and release the subtle vapor held within the nerve-centers that correspond to the Planet within the Alchemist. Coagulation will naturally follow.

The Planetary Incantations

as found in the *Picatrix*
(translated by Christopher Warnock and John Michael Greer)

Saturn

"Oh exalted Lord whose name is great and who stands above the heaven of every other Planet, whom God made subtle and exalted! You are the lord Saturn, who is cold and dry, shadowy, the author of the good, faithful in your friendships, true to your work, durable and persevering in your loves and hatreds; whose knowledge reaches far and deep, truthful in your words and promises, single in your operations, solitary, remote from others, near to suffering and sorrow, far from joy and celebration; you are old, ancient, wise, and you abolish the knowledge of good things; you are the author of good and of evil. Miserable and tormented is he who is made unfortunate by your infortunes and fortunate indeed is he who is touched by your fortunes. In you God has placed powers and virtues, and a spirit causing good and evil. I ask you, father and lord, by your exalted names and wonderful deeds, that you do such and such for me." Prostrate yourself in humility before Saturn.

Jupiter

"May God bless you, Jupiter, blessed Lord, who is the greater fortune, warm and moist, equitable in all your works, affable, beautiful, wise, truthful, Lord of truth and equality, far from all evil, merciful, lover of those who uphold religions and serve them, who thinks little of the things and vices of this world, delighting in religions and religious services, exalted of mind, doer of good and free in your nature, high and honored in your heaven, lawful in your promises and true in the friendships you have. I conjure you first in the name of God Most High who has given you power and spirit, and by your good will and lovely effects, by your noble and precious nature, that you will do such and such for me. For you are the source of all good and goodness, and the maker of all good things. Therefore you hear all petitions that are of goodly form."

For especially theurgic works involving Jupiter use the following incantation:

"God Bless you, noble planet, exalted star, precious and honored! In you God placed powers and spirits that accomplish good, and give form to the bodies of the universe as they appear in the divine law, and give life, and help those who sail the sea, and preserve lives. I ask you, by the strength that God put in you, that you grant your light and spirit to me, whereby I may save myself, and cleanse and purify my nature, so that my perceptions and spirit may be illuminated, so that I may be able to know and understand things."

Mars

"O Mars, you who are an honored Lord and are hot and dry, mighty, weighty, firm of heart, spiller of blood and giver of illnesses thereto! You are strong, hardy, acute, daring, shining, agile and the lord of the battler, pains, miseries, wounds, prisons, sorrows, and mixed and separated things, who has no fear or contemplation of anything, sole helper in all your effects and in investigations thereof, strong in calculation and will to conquer and seek after fortune, cause of lawsuits and battles, doer of evil to the weak and the strong, lover of the sons of battle, vindicator of wicked people and those who do evil in the world. I ask of you and conjure by your names and your qualities that exist in heaven, and by your slayings, and also by your petitions to the Lord God who placed power and strength in you, gathering them in you and separating them from other planets that you might have strength and power, victory over all and great vigor. I conjure you by the High God of the Universe, that you may hear my prayer and attend my petition, and furthermore see my humility and fulfill my petition. I ask that you will do such and such for me." Cut and consume some part of flesh, in Mars' honor.

Sun

"May God bless you, Sun, you who are fortunate and the greater fortune, hot and dry, luminous, resplendent, noble, beautiful, exalted, and honored king over all the stars and planets. Power of beauty, subtlety, good disposition, truth, wisdom, knowledge and riches, which by your virtue are acquired, and in you are made strong. You are the lord of the six planets, which are governed by your motion, and you reign over them and have kingship and lordship over them all. You are king, and they are vassals. You give light and power to them all, and they receive fortunate influences from you and do fortunate things when they aspect you with a favorable aspect, and when they aspect you with an unfortunate aspect, they lose their fortunate influences and become infortunes. No one can possibly perceive all your good and noble qualities, which are infinite to our intellects."

Venus

May God bless you, O Venus, you who are queen and fortune, and are cold and moist, equitable in your effects and complexion, pure and lovely and sweetly scented, beautiful and ornate. You are the lady of adornment, of gold and silver; you delight in love, joy, ornaments and jests, elegance, songs and music that are sung or played on strings, written music and songs played on organs, games and comforts, rest and love. In your effects you remain equal. You take delight in wine, rest, joy, lying with women, for in all of these your natural effects consist. I invoke you by all your names; Venus, Anyhyt, Aphrodite, Sarca. I conjure you by the lord God, the lord of the highest firmament, and by the obedience you offer to God, and by the power and lordship He has over you, that you listen to my prayer and consider my petition. And I conjure you by Beyteyl, who is that angel whom God has set beside you to complete all your powers and effects.

Mercury

"May God bless you, good Lord Mercury, you who are truthful, perceptive, intelligent, and the sage and instructor of every kind of writing, arithmetic, computation, and science of heaven and earth! You are a noble lord and temperate in your joys, and the lord and sustainer and subtle interpreter of wealth, business, money, and profound perceptions. You are the dispositor and significator of prophecy and prophets and their perceptions, reasoning and doctrine, apprehending diverse sciences; of subtlety, intelligence, philosophy, geometry, the sciences of heaven and earth, divination, geomancy and poetry. You are fortunate with fortunes and unfortunate with infortunes, masculine with masculine planets and feminine with feminine planets, you are a helper and a co-worker. I conjure you by the high Lord God, who is the lord of the firmament and of the realm of the exalted and great. I conjure you that you will receive my petition, and grant me that which I ask, and pour out the powers of your spirit upon me, by which I shall be made strong, and my petition granted, and be made apt and disposed to gain knowledge and wisdom."

Say a short and beautiful poem in Mercurius' honor.

Luna

"May God bless you, O Moon, you who are the blessed lady, fortunate, cold and moist, equitable and lovely. You are the chief and key of all the other planets, swift in your motion, having light that shines, lady of happiness and joy, of good words, good reputation, and fortunate realms. You are a lover of the law and a contemplator of the things of this world, subtle in you contemplations. Joy, songs, and jest you take delight in and love; you are the lady of ambassadors and messengers and the concealer of secrets. Free and precious one, you are closer to us than the other planets, you are larger than all and luminous; you are apt to good and evil, you join the planets together and carry their light, and by your goodness you rectify all things. You are the beginning of all things and the end thereof. Thus I call and conjure you by Celan, who is the angel whom God set beside you to complete all your effects, that you will take pity on me and hear my petition."

DISSOLUTION AND PUTREFICATION

THERE ARE TWO RITUALS WE USE TO ENTER INTO THE DISSOLUTION AND Putrefication process: the Death Litany, which is used as part of the daily practice directly after the Antimaquis Rite; and the Death Rite of Saturn, which is a singular ritual used to awaken the Saturnian serpent within the body. The Death Rite of Saturn should be conducted weekly until the force has risen, after which the Adept may use it as he or she sees fit. The Death Litany is a daily tool.

THE DEATH LITANY

First, become aware of your chair and the floor beneath you. Expand your awareness so that it includes both of those things. While holding them in your awareness, state (internally, and not aloud) "THERE IS NO CHAIR, THERE IS ONLY GOD." Say it 3 times. Then for the floor "THERE IS NO FLOOR, THERE IS ONLY GOD". Expand your awareness to include all of the objects you perceive in your room, including the walls, and state "THERE IS NO X, THERE IS ONLY GOD" where X is any "individual" object. Chant this way until you've denied the separate existence of every object you can directly perceive with your eyes. You'll have entered into a very specific kind of trance state, one tuned to the Death-Force. Take a moment to note what you perceive. Now, perform the Litany on everything that you hear within the room, and everything you smell. Next, concentrate your awareness on your own body, and destroy it limb by limb. Turn your attention inward, and think of the things you Love. Your job, your wife/husband/partner, your children, your parents. Hold each in your mind, and then destroy them. This part can be difficult, but it must be done as well. Take up the things you hate, and destroy them as well. The chant will have a Power at this point, a momentum. Let it roll through and destroy everything that you know, every thought that arises, until your mind is Quiet. Now destroy yourself: "THERE IS NO X, THERE IS ONLY GOD", where X is the name you most identify with. All of the things that are you, are lost in God, the veil of the Salt-Force lifted, the illusion of separation weakened. Sit quietly in awareness of the blackness around you, and lose yourself in it.

KAMEA OF SATURN

PREPARATIONS

The initiate must avoid sexual contact for 3 days before the rite. This isn't arbitrary; the Desire-Force that is centered in the Mars center fuels the rising of the Serpent from the Saturn center. This Inner Fire is used repeatedly in the Alchemical work. This Rite shouldn't be completed by persons new to Alchemy and Magic; it should only be conducted after a person has had a year of experience. That being said, everyone develops at a different level. Use divination to determine the best time for this Rite for yourself.

The initiate must refrain from eating any foods three hours before performing the rite. Digestion takes primacy in our physical forms (because it's required to fuel life), and the body directs its resources toward handling digestion first. Being sated (not starving!) but also not actively digesting makes a huge difference in coaxing the various Serpents to rise. They rarely do so on a full stomach. This is why, for myself, the rising didn't occur until I'd finished digesting and after I'd slept. Once you've begun the Litany, the force Will Rise, and will keep trying to rise until you create the conditions necessary for it to do so. Don't approach the rite half-assed. The requirements are not difficult. Meet them.

It is best if you've taken a nap before doing the ritual. You'll be lying down for some of it, and you'll be less likely to fall asleep during the meditative portion if you are fully rested.

About midway through the Rite you will perform the Death Litany of Saturn, which is the incantation we use to destroy our world and rest in

Putrefication. The Death Litany alone is used during our Daily Practice; the Death Rite of Saturn is used as a separate rite for raising the death-force and acquiring the Black Powder state. Once the state has been acquired, the Death Rite need only be performed annually, although weekly would be best.

Tools:

This rite should be performed without clothing. You'll see why as you read the ritual itself.

Kamea of Saturn
Image of Saturn
Saturnian incense
Black Candle
Pillow

Astrological Timing:

The absolute best time to perform this ritual is when Saturn is in his Exaltation and Retrograde, during the Hour of Saturn on the Day of Saturn after Sunset with a Waning moon. If that can't be achieved, the bare minimum requirement is during the Hour of Saturn on the Day of Saturn, with the Sun having set and the Moon Waning. It will work just fine with the minimum requirement, but having Saturn at his strongest and most Destructive is a powerful aid, especially if the initiate hasn't risen any of the Inner Fires before.

The Rite:

Begin with a ritual purification, using Holy Water (that you've made yourself) after you've taken a bath. Wash your head, your heart, and your genitalia (including your perineum) with it.

Create the Tower of Art, and perform the Holy Yeheshuah rite.

Place the Candle atop the Kamea of Saturn, light it, and perform the Antimaquis Rite.

Summary of Saturnian names and prayer for use during the Rite:

Godname: Yehovah Elohim

Internal Metal: The Perineum/Perineal Ganglia

The Spirits:
Coadunate: Redemiz
Above: Toz
Below: Corez
Right: Deytyz
Left: Deriuz
Behind: Daruz
Spirit of Motion through the Heavens: Tahaytuc
Before: Talyz

Prayer to Saturn, as found in the *Picatrix*:

"Oh exalted Lord whose name is great and stands above the heaven of every other planet, whom God made subtle and exalted! You are the lord Saturn, who is cold and dry, shadowy, the author of the good faithful in your friendships, true to your work, durable and persevering in your loves and hatreds; whose knowledge far and deep, truthful in your words and promises, single in your operations, solitary, remote from others, near to suffering and sorrow, far from joy and celebration; you are old ancient, wise, and you abolish the knowledge of good things; you are the author of good and evil. Miserable and tormented is he who is made unfortunate by your infortunes and fortunate indeed is he who is touched by your fortunes. In you God has placed powers and virtues, and a spirit causing good and evil. I ask you, father and lord, by your exalted names and wonderful deeds, that you do "*such and such" for me."

*For this Rite, "such and such" should be "Awaken the Serpent of Death and new Life within my form."

Prostrate yourself in humility before Saturn.

Now, sit in the Throne position, and take in your surroundings. You are going to begin the Death Litany, which is a chant done to destroy the world around you, and then yourself, until all of the things that are you are lost in God, the veil of the Salt-Force has been lifted, and the illusion of separation weakened.

Lay down in the fetal position now, and place your awareness within the perineum. This is very important; the pressure placed on the perineum while sitting makes it difficult to isolate and perceive it. Lay on the earth, like a child.

With your awareness on the perineum, which contains the nerve-force of Saturn and is the home of the Death-Serpent, begin the Bellows breath. This is a slow breath – so slow that it makes no sound – that we use in our Alchemy to stoke the Inner Fire. Keep your awareness on the Saturn-center, and stoke the Fire, until you perceive a tingling or throbbing in the center. Now take up the Death Litany, and incant "There IS NO I, THERE IS ONLY GOD." Do this while performing the Bellows-Breath as long as you can, with eyes closed. When you tire, release the incantation and behold the blackness in your mind. Allow yourself to fall asleep.

When you awaken, write down any dreams you have.

At any point after the Bellows-Breathing begins, the Serpent may rise. It is different for everyone. It may happen immediately during the ritual, it may happen on the train ride in to work the next day. Once the Rite is performed, to stimulate the Serpent-force you can perform the Death-litany wherever you find yourself, in combination with the Bellows-breath. You will know it has happened when it does.

RITUALS FOR INCINERATION AND MULTIPLICATION

These operations are the work of Nature; all that is required of the Alchemist who has properly prepared by working regularly the Purification, Calcination, Sublimation, Coagulation, Dissolution, and Putrefication processes is prayer. The Alchemist enflames himself with prayer, and the heavens burn in sympathy. It will happen sometimes spontaneously, sometimes it requires months of deep and earnest prayer. Even after Incineration is complete, and the heavenly part has entered into the Mercury, making it pregnant, continued calcination is necessary to grow a healthy and strong Child. This new person is the revitalized Alchemist, who has conquered death.

The Death that is conquered isn't physical death – Alchemists still die. Just so we're clear on that. They inhabit heavenly bodies that allow them to continue as they are into the next world, instead of having their parts sent back into the Azoth and being reborn anew. This is the fate we have all suffered in previous existences, as the seed did not truly sprout in our lifetimes. The Alchemical process aims to assist nature in her refining process, and give the Alchemist a chance at conscious immortality.

THE DAILY PRACTICE

1. Perform the Purification Rites

2. Perform the general Calcination rite for the First Matter (The Holy Yeheshua Rite).

3. If prepared, ingest Spagyric Elixir for the Planet being worked with (instruction for creating these is found in the Book of the Blossoming Flower, at the end of this book.) It is important that the plant be taken through the entire Spagyric process delineated in the attached Book of the Blossoming Flower. The internal Metal will be in sympathy with the consumed Elixir; the more refined the elixir, the more positive the effect on the Metal (which we are refining into a purer state, into Gold).

Perform the Lemnian Fire Rite. This rite is the heart of the practice; it is important that it be performed regularly and consistently.

Perform the heating of the individual Metals as is appropriate for the Day (The Antimaquis Rite.) This Rite is done for the Metal that is appropriate for the Planetary Hour in which the Alchemist is working. The Planetary Day is important, but is not as important as the Hour. This allows for some flexibility, as situations that occur in life may make having both Day and Hour difficult.

4. Perform the Death Litany, and enter into Dissolution and from there Putrefication. Lose yourself in this state for as much time as possible, but for a minimum of seven breaths.

5. Give thanks to the entities that are assisting in the process, with especial thanks to the Spirits of the Planet worked with during the Antimaquis Rite.

6. Say a short heartfelt prayer to the ineffable One, to Azoth, for completion of the Great Work and the birth and growth of your Soul.

7. Seal the Vessel with the Solar Cross Ritual, so that the Matter continues to Calcine under Hermetic Seal as you go about your mundane day.

That's it. It's simple, but it works. It only requires consistency and prayer. This is Kameothic Internal Alchemy. It is an Amalgam Way, meaning a combination of the Wet and Dry alchemical processes. The Dry Alchemy involves using a hot external fire, and the Wet way uses a slower Inner fire. Our way uses the un-natural external fire to stoke the Inner fire. (Interestingly enough, in External Alchemy the Dry Way – with its extremely hot external fire – is much faster than the Wet Way. Internal Alchemy is the opposite; the Wet way directly stimulating the Inner Fire is much faster than the Dry Way.) Some of the rituals that are rooted in the Golden Dawn/RR et AC tradition are used in different ways within this Ordo than in their root Orders. This isn't an interpretation of what those Orders intended for those particular rituals; they are used in this way simply because they work for the purposes outlined. They may work for entirely different purposes in other systems.

THE
BOOK
OF THE
BLOSSOMING FLOWER

THIS IS A MODEST WORK ON THE ART OF HEALING USING SPAGYRIC AND CEREMONIAL TECHNIQUE, TO EASE SUFFERING.

THEORY AND METHOD

There is a deep, profound need for healing in our Western society that addresses more than just the physical form – that is holistic, and considers the energetic and mental well-being of the Entire person. The roots of disease are understood, by many, to be spiritual; treating disease from a purely physical standpoint only treats the final affect of the problem without addressing its root cause. This continued energetic imbalance/disharmony may then manifest again within the body at a later date. To be effective, we treat the entire person – the physical body, the energetic body, and the emotional/mental bodies.

It is important to understand that the methods used to effect positive change upon the energies all have some effect on every level. The levels themselves are somewhat illusory – refer to the Hermetic Axiom for understanding of why that is.

None of these methods of treatment exist in isolation. What affects the physical body sends reverberations within, and what affects the mental and energetic body sends reverberations throughout the entire person as well. By consciously working on all three levels, we hope to create a state of energetic balance and well being that encourages serenity and health within the person.

SPAGERY

Our primary tool for creating healing within a person is the western Alchemical art of Spagery. Spagery itself is a technique used to evolve a plant and its essence into a higher state, and to evolve one's self through consumption and use of that evolved material. The techniques of Spagery refine the plant's body and purify and concentrate its energies, until its final form is pure and rich with the Spirit of the thing.

Spagyric potions make fine medicines for a holistic treatment, as they work on the deeper levels where the root of disease often lies. Spagery is a complicated art rife with mystery, but can be simple and straightforward once one understands the keys to making it work. One singularly important key to Spagery lies in the Awareness, and this is the same key the profane need to open the mysteries of Energy Work and Ceremonial Magic. We have to use our awareness to learn to manipulate energy, and then apply that same awareness to our work with Spagery, so that we can sense and feel the process of evolution, and take part in it. For the Spagyrist with a proper sense of Awareness, what happens to the plant's energies also happens to himself – he connects to the plant using that awareness, and so transforms every act of the Spagyric process into an act of magic that helps in his own transformation.

Spagyric potions are also particularly useful in that the evolutionary process inherent in Spagery enhances the natural medicinal qualities of the plant itself. While in this manuscript a number of different ideas are put forward as to combining Spagery with Ceremonial Magic, Spagery alone serves as a fine healing method. The addition of the Ceremonial, and the special tools, rituals and meditations, are about enhancing and directing the already refined healing energies intrinsic to the Spagyric potions, be they tincture or elixir.

The Spagyric methods given here are extremely simple; these methods are a baseline, the bare minimum needed to make Spagyric products. They are by no means more than elementary methods. The Spagyric process can be exceedingly precise, and requires a deep study and plenty of lab equipment to master. To further develop your Spagery, read Frater Albertus' *Practical Handbook of Plant Alchemy*, and apply the lessons learned there. You will find detailed information about equipment and processes that are not mentioned in this manuscript.

THE GARDEN

In order to be effective and useful the Alchemical healer will need to have Spagyric products on hand to help heal the persons in need he encounters – imagine having to wait a week for the pharmacist to hand-prepare aspirin to treat a headache. This collection of plants, tinctures, Elixirs, incense and Unda Superum is called a Garden. The Garden should contain a full range of Spagyric products related to the Elements/Planets/

Signs in addition to basic herbs with qualities used to treat physical discomfort and injury. For example, my Garden contains Basil because it corresponds to Elemental Fire, and Violet because it is Elemental Water, and Aloe Vera because it is useful for treating burns and cuts, regardless of its metaphysical properties. It does not take a massive collection of plants to treat the basic physical discomforts, or to treat a myriad of energetic and mental issues. It is best to have a Garden that contains plants that fill multiple roles. A Garden should contain a plant to fight infection, to combat burns, to relieve pain, and to soothe digestion, in addition to any metaphysical properties those plants may have. This way, minor physical problems may be treated immediately and a person's pain reduced.

The Spagyrist's Tools

The following is a list of basic items the spagyrist will need to do his work. I have chosen the simplest, easiest to acquire tools that I could arrange to create a basic, semi-portable laboratory. There are more refined tools one can use to create a more refined product; I will leave this to the individual spagyrist. The laboratory and Garden shown here is the simple one I used myself to create tinctures, elixirs, and the Unda Superum when I began to practice Spagery. There are far more refined setups one can use, with distillation trains and the like (and I wholeheartedly recommend them), after you've made a full range of products (completed a Garden) and proven yourself capable of using the elementary setup. Lab glass ain't cheap – you will thank me later.

Materials

Mortar and Pestle (For grinding Salts)

Collection of Herbs

Mason Jars (to serve as Alchemical Vessels)

Small amber-colored laboratory bottles (for storing products)

Pure grain Alcohol (to serve as a simple Mercury)

Grappa, I have experienced, is a better Mercury – feel free to use it if available. The best Mercury to use is the pure alcohol distilled from Red Wine. I've made perfectly serviceable and living products using commonly available 88 proof grain alcohol like Everclear. It isn't the best choice, but it gets the job done and is readily available. Use the best that is available, but don't skip working because you don't have the absolute best at hand.

Retort

Metal Crucible

Receiving Flask

Handheld Torch: The sort used in restaurants. The fuel comes in cans, and is readily available and affordable. One fuel can will burn for two hours continuously, more than enough time to reduce and purify the Plant Salts that we are working with. This takes the place, in my laboratory, of the kiln or the high-temperature oven. The torch's flame is 2300 degrees Fahrenheit at its tip, and has proven itself a valuable tool. I do not own a garage, and must assemble my laboratory on the fly. I've found using a torch useful in that it forces one to attend to the calcination of the Salts personally and actively, instead of sticking them in the kiln and then moving on.

Distilled Water: We can create this ourselves with the retort. Purified substances should be combined with purified water for leeching/consumption.

Wooden cutting board

Small Knife (Used only for Spagery, and marked with the unified Alchemical sign.)

Trunk or Apothecary's cabinet or armoire for storing the Garden and Tools (IKEA is your friend, here.)

Cloth for cleaning

Small shallow dish

Coffee Filters

These things are all relatively easy to obtain, and shouldn't cost more than a couple hundred dollars, if one is careful in purchasing. One could easily spend thousands of dollars creating a Garden and a laboratory; these tools are utilitarian and simple, but with the application of Intent, Awareness, and hard work, they will get the job done.

SPAGYRIC ALCHEMICAL SYMBOLS

Salt: This refers to the physical body of the plant, both refined and unrefined.

Mercury: This refers to the transferative medium, that which carries the Spirit (Sulfur), and mediates between it and the Salt. In Spagery, this refers to the alcohol; however, in Spagery Mercury is not exactly the alcohol/oil within which we suspend the herb. The true Mercury is the subtle vapor that rises from the gross liquid during the warming/cooling process within the hermetically sealed jar, carrying the sulfur with it into the "heavens" while it is warm and rejoining with the base liquid as it cools. This vapor is the Child of the Sun and the Moon – produced by the action of heat upon moisture – and carried within the Air, which is the receptacle within which the vapor rises and falls. This Mercury can be lifted from, and exists within, all things, but is most easily separated from liquid. We use alcohol as a medium because of its penetrative qualities.

Sulfur: This refers to the pure spirit, the heaven within the earth. Sulfur is the true essence of the plant, mineral, or person, and it can be extracted from a plant with the use of base Mercury (alcohol).

Mercury and Sulfur are two poles of the same essence. With the circulations and the purifications and the application of subtle heat that occurs inside the vessel during the Sublimation process, the Mercury itself is refined into more subtle Sulfur. I believe this to be the reason that the Spagyric Alchemical process greatly increases the purity and efficacy of a plant – all of its parts (Salt, Mercury, Sulfur) are refined, but the ratio of Sulfur to the other parts is greatly increased due to the exaltation of Mercury into Sulfur (Multiplication), creating something that is much stronger in Spirit than its non-evolved counterpart.

I am by no means the final word on this subject. Trust your own understanding, if you find it differs from my own.

THE SPAGYRIC ALCHEMICAL PROCESS

Mortification: This is the initial death, destruction, and dismemberment of the plant, and is the beginning of the Spagyric Alchemical process. Here we have plucked the plant, chopped it fine and ground it down; it is unrecognizable as the plant it once was, and is now suitable for further evolution. It is completed after the Sublimation phase, when the Sulfur and Mercury are separated from the Salt of the plant body.

Sublimation: Air. That which is of low vibration is translated into higher vibration, and the hidden spirit within matter is released. In Spagery, this refers to the portion of the process when we extract the Sulfur from a plant using the gross Mercury and the subtle heating/cooling-expansion/contraction... breathing... within the alchemical vessel (the mason jar). At the end of this process, upon separating the Salt from the Mercury/Sulfur, the remaining liquid is a Tincture.

Calcination: Fire. This is the action of heating the matter that has undergone the Mortification (having had its Sulfur and Mercury separated from it during the Sublimation Phase) to whiten and purify it, fundamentally raising its vibration.

Dissolution: Water. The solid matter disappears into water – the Earth is swallowed by the sea. In Spagery, this is the part where the calcined salts are dissolved into distilled Water, and the Caput Mortum (the Death's Head, the filtered matter that is insoluble and remains in the Filter after the combined distilled water and calcined Salts are poured through a filter) is discarded. This is the beginning of the leeching process.

Coagulation: The salt that has been dissolved into the liquid is reborn/reappears after the water evaporates. This is the final part of the leeching process. Having been purified by water, that salt is allowed to return as an evolved body by the evaporation of the liquid solution.

Conjunction: Earth. The re-combination of the spirit and the refined body, the re-birth, the resurrection. In Spagery, this is where we dissolve salt into the tincture, to create an Elixir. This is a holy thing, and should be treated as such.

PROCESSES AND PRODUCTS

HERE IS A STEP-BY-STEP METHOD FOR PRODUCTION OF EACH OF THE NECESSARY Spagyric Products.

MAKING A SPAGYRIC TINCTURE

1. Take up your plant, and on the Day/Hour corresponding to the energy you wish to refine (Planet, Element, or Sign), chop the plant into fine pieces on your cutting board, beginning the Mortification stage. Sunrise on the Day corresponding to a planet is best – for astrological forces. I had success capturing the Astrological powers by beginning the work when the Sign is in the Ascendant, preferably during an Elemental Tide that corresponds to the Triplicity the Sign is associated with. For Elemental powers, I have found that beginning the work during an Elemental Tide for the force is efficacious.

2. Place the chopped plant matter (unrefined Salt) into the mortar, and grind it down with the pestle, continuing the Mortification of the Plant.

3. Place the unrefined Salt into the mason jar (which will serve as our Alchemical Vessel). Cover the Salt, with an inch of liquid to spare, with the pure Alcohol. This is our Mercury. Be sure that at least half of the mason jar is left empty of all but air. The spirit has to have Air in which to be carried. Seal the jar, so that nothing may enter or exit it.

4. Cover the mason jar in black cloth or Aluminum foil, and leave it somewhere outside where it will not be disturbed for one week; I believe it is important to subject the potion to the natural heating and cooling of the environment for the Sublimation phase. Waiting longer than a week (a month) will give you a stronger tincture, although it is more important, in my opinion, to get your Garden set up and working at this point than to concern yourself with having the most powerful substances. Better to have

something on hand, when it is needed, than to have something in a Jar that is unprepared, and be unable to help yourself or someone else. One week is enough for them to work well, although a Lunar month is the best. We'll get the Garden set up first, and then concern ourselves with refining more powerful medicines with which to treat ourselves and our kin.

5. The Sublimation phase will occur within the hermetically sealed alchemical vessel at this point. During the week, as the potion heats, the subtle Mercury will rise from the gross Mercury, carrying with it the Sulfur, and then recombine with the gross Mercury (the Alcohol) – in more rarified form – as it cools. This will happen in a continuous cycle (the Ouroboros), and so we have begun to separate the fixed from the flying, the Eagle from the Toad.

6. Now, after the week has passed, remove the covering and open the mason jar. You will see that the gross mercury has darkened in color; this is a sign that the Sulfur of the plant has been extracted into the Mercury. Using a funnel and a coffee filter (fine lab filters are, of course, preferable, but coffee filters work well and are readily available), pour the potion into a container, leaving the Salt behind in the filter. The liquid Mercury remaining is your Tincture.

7. Place the Tincture into your retort and, on a low heat, distill the spirit into a Receiving flask. Re-combine the liquids and repeat six times, for a total of seven. Perform the distillations at the appropriate hour. As the Spirit flies, it becomes more refined, and its efficacy is increased.

The key to making this medicine powerful is to use your awareness and involve yourself in the process. Meditate upon the steps of the process as they occur, and use the images that appear within your mind's eye to create Alchemical Emblems of your own. If you wish to perform the refining process of Spagery on your own energies, perform the Sign of the Enterer, creating a link between yourself and the plant, before beginning the Mortification phase. This is a Lunar and analogical magic. Perform the Sign of Silence, and incorporate the Spagyric gear within your Sphere of Sensation. Strive to feel the changes occurring to your energies as you alter the plant's energy and refine it. Take time each day as the plant undergoes Sublimation to meditate upon the process, and strive to feel that same circulation within your own sphere. Perform the Sign of Silence again after the process is complete, and seal the medicine within one of your dark glass bottles (glass, because it is non-reactive, and dark so that the external energies don't affect the purity of the Tincture). Take a dose of the elixir each day during the appropriate hour for the force involved, gently refining your energies.

MAKING SPAGYRIC OILS

The process for making Oils is the same as the process for making Tinctures; one simply substitutes a quality cold-pressed olive oil for the Alcohol. However, Oils will take at least a month in Sublimation before they are ready, as the oil does not have the penetrative quality of the alcohol and needs more time to draw out the Sulfur and Mercury of the plant. Also, we do not make the oil "fly" in the retort; we simply calcine the Plant body until it is white, apply the dissolution technique, and then re-combine the leeched salts of the plant with the oil.

MAKING SPAGYRIC ELIXIRS

The process used for making Elixirs begins with the process for creating tinctures. We will re-create that process, and add the new elements at step 7 below.

1. Take up your plant, and on the Day/Hour corresponding to the energy you wish to refine (Planet, Element, or Sign), chop the plant into fine pieces on your cutting board, beginning the Mortification stage. Sunrise on the Day corresponding to a planet is best – for astrological forces. I prefer to capture and refine the Astrological powers by beginning the work when the Sign is in the Ascendant, preferably during an Elemental Tide that corresponds to the Triplicity the Sign is associated with. For Elemental powers, I have found that beginning the work during an Elemental Tide for the force is efficacious.

2. Place the chopped plant matter (unrefined Salt) into the mortar, and grind it with the pestle until its form is uniform, continuing the Mortification of the Plant.

3. Place the unrefined Salt into the mason jar (which will serve as our Alchemical Vessel). Cover the Salt with an inch of liquid above its topmost part, with the pure grain Alcohol. Be sure that at least half of the mason jar is left empty of all but air. The Spirit needs Air to carry it, so that it can later be born into the Salt once more. Seal the jar, so that nothing may enter or exit it.

4. Cover the mason jar in Aluminum foil, and leave it somewhere outside where it will not be disturbed for one week; I believe it is important to subject the potion to the natural heating and cooling of the environment for the Sublimation phase. Waiting longer than a week (a month) will give you a stronger tincture, although it is more important, in my opinion, to get your Garden set up and working at this point than to concern yourself with having the most powerful substances. Better to have something on hand when it is needed than to have something in a Jar that is unprepared, and be unable to help someone. One week is enough for them to work, and work well.

5. The Sublimation phase will occur within the hermetically sealed alchemical vessel at this point. During the week, as the potion heats, the subtle Mercury will rise from the gross Mercury, carrying with it the Sulfur, and then recombine with the gross Mercury (the Alcohol) as it cools, which has extracted the Sulfur from the plant matter. This will happen in a continuous cycle, and so we have begun to separate the fixed from the flying, the Eagle from the Toad.

6. Now, after the week has passed, remove the covering and open the mason jar. You will see that the gross mercury has darkened in color – this is a sign that the Sulfur of the plant has been extracted into the Mercury. Using a funnel and a coffee filter (fine lab filters are, of course, preferable, but coffee filters work well and are readily available), pour the potion into a container, leaving the Salt behind in the filter. Seal this Tincture and place it close by.

7. Take up that Salt and place it into the metal crucible. We are going to begin the Calcination process, during which Fire is applied to the Salts to refine them as much as possible. Using the Torch (I recommend placing the metal crucible in a bowl filled with sand, so that excess heat

is dispersed safely), burn the Salts until they are dry, black, and charred. This is their Putrefaction. Use tongs to lift the crucible, and pour the black Salts into the Mortar. Grind them down into a fine black ash with the pestle, and then return them to the crucible. This is the Black Powder. Burn the Salts again, calcining them until they begin to turn grey-white. Return them to the Mortar, and grind them down. Repeat this process until you end up with a light-gray to white colored Salt. You will find that Calcination greatly decreases the amount of Salt you have. It is efficacious to use a second plant of the exact same type, and calcine it as well, to give you a greater store of the Salt to work with.

8. Now, we will purify the Salts with Water, using a technique called Leeching. This is the Dissolution step in the Spagyric process. Take a small amount of Distilled water (you can distill tap water or spring water yourself, using your Retort, to remove most of the impurities; pure rain water, caught before it touches the ground so that it is both Virginal and Pregnant with the Solar Sulfur works best) and dissolve the Salts into it. Stir for a couple of minutes and then, taking up the funnel and coffee filter again, pour the combination into a shallow dish. Whatever Salt is left in the funnel is insoluble in water, and is referred to in Spagery as the Caput Mortum, the Death's Head. Discard this truly dead matter. Place this dish where it will get some sun – and be otherwise undisturbed – and let it evaporate. Subtle heat may be applied to speed the process. As the water evaporates, the purified Salt body will appear. This is the Coagulation phase. This salt will be white, and should be ground once more in the mortar so that it is fine, if it is not fine already.

9. This final step is the Conjunction phase, where the refined and purified Sulfur, Mercury, and Salt of the plant are recombined – here we marry the Fixed to the Flying. Take up the tincture, and slowly dissolve the Salt into it, until they are once again one body. This is a holy moment, creating a holy thing, and should be treated as such.

10. The Elixir should be stored in a sealed, glass container, marked with its source plant and planetary/elementary/astrological symbol, and treated with reverence.

CREATING THE UNDA SUPERUM

THE UNDA SUPERUM (WATER OF THE GODS) IS A SPAGYRIC ELIXIR FURTHER enlivened and tuned by Ceremonial Magic. Creating the Unda Superum is straightforward. One creates an Elixir, and then, during the appropriate Hour for the force that the Elixir embodies, one uses either the Antimaquis rite or the Holy Yeheshuah Rite to infuse the Elixir with tuned energies using the Sign of the Enterer. This changes the Elixir into a consumable Talisman.

The Godform of Imhotep is assumed after the Invocation of the Highest Divine Self, instead of the standard Godform for the force that is usually invoked. Imhotep is a God who was once a man, a great physician in ancient Egypt. He is the only commoner ever raised to godhood in that tradition. I find he is a perfect force to work with for our purpose, as he is dedicated explicitly to the healing of his fellow man. It is also good to work with him in that, by invoking him, we make it clear that the ritual is built around and for healing.

I prefer to charge the Unda Superum with the general task of refining and balance the corresponding energy within the person that consumes it, and then targeting the specific disease during the healing ritual. As these rituals are performed under the auspice of the Higher Self, this charging has the added benefit of ensuring a benevolent medicine – energetically, that is. Do not do anything so foolish as to make an elixir out of some deadly plant. Do your research! As an added safeguard, no Spagyric Healer should treat someone with a potion he hasn't first used upon himself.

This may prove to be a boon of great value, as the directed use of the medicine may be broad or exact, depending upon the desires of the spagyrist. We can create the Unda Superum and direct it to heal, to balance – perhaps even to Initiate. (Not into a tradition, but into the sphere/realm of a given force.) It may be used to induce visions, and becomes a wonderful assistant in scrying.

We use it as an aid to Calcination in the Ordo Octopi Nigri Pulveri; the refined plant Spirit works gently upon its Mineral cousins within the Earth, lifting them through sympathy.

The Unda Superum may also be created using the Living Incantation method of the Ordo Octopi Nigri Pulveri. This method is only taught to Adepts of the White phase in the Order.

SCRYING THE UNDA SUPERUM

Scrying is a wonderful way to test the power of the Unda Superum. Sit in silence in your temple/laboratory, and perform the Four-fold Breath. With your mind clear, state internally and externally your desire to travel in the Spirit to the realm within the Unda Superum. Rub a bit of the Unda Superum between your eyes, on your brow. Create the Tower of Art, and then perform the Holy Yeheshuah Rite. Visions and Mental/Astral projections are greatly reliant on the amount of LVX one has available – the more you hold, the greater the clarity and depth of your vision. Raise a large amount of LVX before each scrying attempt and you will, from what I have experienced, have much greater success. Sit down after performing the aforementioned rituals, and consume the prepared Unda Superum with some distilled water. Perform the Bellows-Breath, and when you are completely relaxed, allow images to appear in your mind's eye. Do not grasp them.

Simply note what you see/taste/feel/hear and compare with your correspondences after the ritual. If you have been careful and conscientious in your preparations, you will not be disappointed. This isn't the classic scrying technique used in the Golden Dawn; the consumption of the Unda Superum takes place instead of the Invocatory Rituals, and should be more than enough to tune you in to the energies of the Sphere in question... if your Superum was made correctly.

THE ART OF SPAGYRIC HEALING

NOW THAT WE HAVE A BASIC UNDERSTANDING OF SPAGERY AND THE TOOLS necessary to practice it, we can delve into the practice of healing. As stated before, Spagyric healing works on the entirety of the person, addressing the Salt, Mercury, and Sulfur, which in this instance refers to the physical body, energy bodies, and mind/soul of the recipient. In order to have a positive effect on all three of these levels, the Spagyrist must use techniques that work on each level directly. Our tools are Meditation, Spagery, and Herbalism.

When we conduct the Ritual of Healing, we work on all three levels – we use the Book of Images to work directly upon the mental/emotional, the Unda Superum on the Energetic, and Oils and Poultices on the Physical. When the issue has no discernable physical manifestation (such as, say, depression, or a feeling of inadequacy), apply oil to an appropriate part of the physical body corresponding to the Energy being balanced, in addition to the use of the Unda Superum and Book of Images. Simply use the fingers to draw the symbol of the force upon the body using the Spagyric Oil corresponding to the force. When dealing with what seem to be purely physical problems, you will still conduct a full Ritual of Healing; there is always an energetic root to a physical issue. Use divination and common sense to determine that root, and perform the Ritual accordingly.

TREATING AT THE PHYSICAL LEVEL: BASIC HERBALISM

In the name of efficiency, the Plants listed in the Garden I have created are made up of common, mostly easy to find plants that have well known planetary/elemental/zodiacal attributions and useful herbal correspondences as well. For example, Basil is a Fiery Plant, under the rulership of Mars, that is also an anti-depressant with anti-inflammatory properties. We could use a tincture of basil – applied through the skin via a wet poultice – to treat someone suffering from arthritic pains in their joints, and then have them consume an Unda Superum to help alleviate the spiritual conditions at the root of the ailment.

LEVEL	METHOD
Mind/Emotion/Spirit	Meditation on the Alchemical Icon Incantation Ritual
Energetic Body	Consumption of Tinctures, Elixirs and the Unda Superum
Physical Body	Use of Herbs/plants with known healing properties, according to the Tables of Correspondence. Application of Wet and Dry Poultices, Oils, Teas.

Conditions treated with/rooted in Elemental Fire:	Conditions treated with/rooted in Elemental Water:
Inflammatory Illnesses (such as Arthritis), Stress, Fever, colds and 'flus	Nervousness, Nightmare, Sinus illnesses, cold sores, circulatory issues, painful menstruation, tiredness, sexual issues, Depression
Conditions treated with/rooted in Elemental Air:	Condition treated with/rooted in Elemental Earth:
High blood pressure, poor clotting, weak immune system, circulatory issues	General Pain, fungal issues, headache, stiffness, indigestion

Using the extremely simple chart above (which I've constructed by pairing the elemental designation of common herbs with the conditions they have been classically used to treat) and the basic Garden, a practicing Alchemical Healer could alleviate many of the common physical discomforts one would encounter.

Generally, we would use Elemental powers for treating Physical issues, Astrological powers for the Personality issues, and Planetary powers for treating external/life issues.

Charts detailing the assignations of the Signs and Planets to their respective areas of influence are readily available on the internet.

With Herbalism, the possibilities are literally endless – with research, one can discover a specific herb that is useful for treating a specific illness and, by using careful divination, determine the correct correspondence for the plant involved. This, however, is only for the extremely dedicated healer. For those of us who wish to have a handy tool to alleviate pain and heal the common diseases one encounters, the above will prove to be more than enough, in practice. Why have ten different plants to accomplish a task, when one will do? This manuscript is a simple one, and is an attempt at creating a baseline. Feel free to delve deeper into Herbalism or Spagery or Ritual Magic as you wish, as this will only broaden your abilities as a healer.

TREATING PERSONALITY ISSUES

To treat issues one has with Personality – nullifying negative traits one may have acquired, or adding positive traits one needs to have a balanced life and Personality – we use the astrological Signs. For example, if a person were lacking in initiative, and found this to be having a negative effect on his life, we would treat with the Unda Superum for the Sign of Aries. The Ritual of Healing would consist primarily of the application of an Oil of Aries, consumption of the Arian Unda Superum, and meditation upon the symbol of Ares within the Book of Images, paired with the Incantation (which is a stylized, repeating form of the Statement of Intent).

HOW TO CREATE A POULTICE

The poultice is useful in that it allows us to topically deliver Spagyric potions to persons in need, delivering directed healing to specific areas of concern. By using the Poultice, in combination with Spagyric potions, we are able to treat immediately painful diseases such as burns, rashes, or inflamed joints, and address their energetic components at the same time.

Generally, only tinctures should be used in the Poultices. The Elixirs and the Unda Superum are both to be treated as spiritual beings, and one should not risk a drop of them going to waste. However, in situations where the person in need is unable to do the full Healing Ritual, an Elixir may be used instead of a tincture. Its greater spiritual refinement will help it penetrate further beyond the physical level than the tincture would with a topical application.

Creating a poultice is quite simple. Moisten a folded piece of clean cotton with the tincture you will be using. Create a paste with the Herb being used (grind it in the mortar and pestle, and add some water) and apply this paste to the prepared cotton cloth. Place this mixture over the area to be treated, sealing it off with a wrapped cloth, or cover it with plastic food wrap and tape the edges off. This is for a cold poultice - it can be made warm by soaking the cloth initially in a hot tea of the herb being used for healing.

Obviously, do not use this method on persons who have experienced major physical trauma. They need to see a physical doctor. Subtle cures aren't for this kind of illness. Be sure to ascertain whether the person being worked with has any allergies before using your Elixirs.

THE TOOLS OF THE ALCHEMICAL HEALER

THERE ARE SPECIFIC TOOLS THAT I HAVE DEVELOPED TO ASSIST IN THE SPAGYRIC Healing Ritual. Each tool's purpose, creation, and use are detailed below.

THE STAFF OF IMHOTEP

The Staff of Imhotep came to me during a moment of intense meditation upon the role and work of the Alchemical Healer. It has, at its heart, the classic Caduceus of Hermes. It has been tuned in such a way as to bring to mind the general principles of Alchemy... and is not having its egregore ridden by the legions of uninitiated persons practicing Western medicine. Imhotep is the God who assists us in the healing work, and he appears to have chosen us as well. The staff differs from the classic Caduceus primarily in the use of Alchemical symbolism and the ascending/descending Triangles of the elements. With this design, we are able to manipulate/contact any of the Forces (Elemental, Astrological, and Planetary) that we use in our work with only one tool that is dedicated to Alchemical work.

Each of the triangles of the elements have the three primary Alchemical symbols drawn within them – Sulfur at the Point, with Mercury and Salt at the base. (These are inscribed clockwise from Sulfur.) The first three triangles, closest to the head of the staff, are Fire and are red, with the alchemical symbols written in green. At the Center of each triangle one of the symbols of Fire's astrological triplicity is drawn, in its own primary color. The Planetary ruler of the Elemental triplicity should be drawn in the middle triangle, above the Astrological sign.

The next set of 3 triangles will be of Elemental Air, and should be Yellow with complimentary Purple (the alchemical signs being drawn in purple). Following the Air triangles are those of Water, and then Earth, with each triangle being painted in accordance with the Element's primary and complimentary colors.

Ribbons of red and blue are wound and tied about the staff, at the Adept's discretion, to symbolize the positive and negative polarities, and the main energetic channels that rise from the base of the spine into the head. Atop the staff is the unified symbol of the Alchemical principles – with joined Sulfur and Mercury atop the orb of Salt.

CONSECRATING THE STAFF OF IMHOTEP

To create and consecrate this staff, first purify the bare and unpainted staff with Holy Water. Assume the Godform of Imhotep. (Meditate upon the name IMHOTEP to receive an image of the God to work with.) Wrap the staff in a thick white cloth, and then, mix the appropriate Unda Superum into the paints that will be used to color it. Lay out the white cloth, and, setting the staff upon it, commence painting it, with reverence, layer by layer, until it is complete. Paint the staff first a pure and shining White. Don't glop on the paint, but paint in thin layers so that once you have finished the first, you may paint the next upon it in a short amount of time. This may take a few hours – it will require some dedication and discipline. So does Alchemical healing. Paint slowly and painstakingly – if you feel yourself rushing, stop for a few minutes, and regain your composure. When you have completed painting the staff, divest yourself of the Godform of Imhotep and leave the temple. Return in a few hours, reassume the Godform, and apply a protective varnish. Give this time to dry, while you meditate on your desire to heal your fellow Man and ease suffering. Create the Tower of Art and perform the Holy Yeheshuah Rite. Draw a circle about the Staff with LVX using your right hand, and within, draw the united Alchemical symbol whilst vibrating strongly "AZOTH". Now, project LVX into the Staff using the Sign of the Enterer. Do so repeatedly until exhausted. Perform the Sign of Silence. Wrap the staff in the cloth upon which it was painted. Use and carry this staff during all of your alchemical work.

THE BOOK OF IMAGES

The Book of Images is a collection of charged pictures used during the meditative component of the Ritual of Healing. It is important for spiritual practitioners to use the Art to reduce suffering when possible, and this small healing system (detailed in the second book of this work, the Book of the Blossoming Flower) is what the Ordo has to offer. Each page holds a simple image charged with the balanced force of a particular Element/Planet/Sign – this charging is done with the Unda Superum, by mixing the appropriate colored paints with it. This creates a book of Talismans, made expressly for the purpose of balancing the energies within the person who meditates upon them and creates a link between themselves and the image via the Sign of the Enterer. The first page and last page of the book are filled with the Holy Image – an Image that represents all of the forces in perfect balance. This is the image the healer meditates upon and links with before conducting the Ritual of Healing. In the Ordo Octopi Nigri Pulveri, we use the image of the Alchemical Dragon.

My book of images is relatively simple – I use a stencil to draw as perfect a circle as possible onto the paper, and then paint the complimentary color of the force as the background within the circle – leaving the rest of the page uncolored. I then paint the classic symbol for the force prominently within the circle – all of this done with the "enlivened" paint. This has worked very well for me, and did not require a large amount of artistic skill. The images, especially if painted using vibrant, flashing colors, are very powerful tools.

Before conducting the Ritual of Healing, during the Ritual of Adoration the Alchemist meditates on an Image representing perfect balance – an image of Azoth, of the Perfect and Whole Macrocosm (for example, the Sigillum Dei Ameth, or the Alchemical Dragon) – and creates a link between himself and this Holy Image using the Sign of the Enterer. This is done so that during the ceremony, the Spagyrist may present a perfectly balanced spiritual body-image – or as close to it as he may come by Art – to interact with that of the recipient of treatment. The Book of Images works by connecting the balanced and evolved energies of the images with the corresponding energies within a person, and raising them through that connection. So, working with the book alone is gentle Analogical Magic, Lunar Magic. Pairing it with consumption of an elixir or Unda Superum, and you work directly upon the matter – that would make this Solar Magic.

THE RITES OF HEALING

These rituals are performed consecutively. The first by the Spagyrist, the second primarily by the person being healed, with the Spagyrist assisting, and the last by the Person being healed alone.

THE RITUAL OF ADORATION

The purpose of this ritual is to prepare the ritual space by cleansing it of unwanted energies, and then charging it with positive, healing energies. It is also where the Spagyrist exalts his mundane self by Invoking his Highest Divine Self, and then dedicates the work to healing with the Invocation of Imhotep. Another important part of this ritual is that it is performed in the space before inviting the recipient of the Healing. The Ritual of Healing is simple and meditative, and is not heavy on the ceremonial magic, which seems strange to some folks and may make them ill at ease. This would work against our magic and the Healing which we are trying to accomplish.

The Ritual of Adoration is as follows:

Purify with Holy Water.

Create the Tower of Art.

State your intent, "That this space might be a pure receptacle of the Holy LVX, and that all within it may be uplifted" or something similarly evocative, with the intent of inviting the higher energies into the space, so that they might exalt the lower energies within us.

Perform the Invocation of the Godform, and Invoke IMHOTEP.

Perform the Holy Yeheshuah Rite.

Perform the Sign of the Enterer upon the Holy Image, and meditate for a short time.

Reverently leave the space, and invite the Recipient inside.

THE RITUAL OF HEALING

This Ritual is simple, and should be performed with a quiet reverence. After preparing the space with the Ritual of Adoration, and Inviting the Recipient inside, the Imhotep stands at the East, and the Recipient to the West of the Table (altar). The Imhotep performs the Sign of the Enterer while holding the Staff of Imhotep, and then the Sign of Silence toward the Recipient.

Upon the Table should be a receptacle holding the healing Oil, a plain wooden cup holding the Unda Superum, and the Book of Images. The Book of Images is open (facing the Recipient) to the appropriate Image for the force being worked with to assist in the healing. Incense corresponding to the force should be burning. The space should be lit by candlelight at night or daylight, never artificial light. There should be a stool or a chair in the East for the Imhotep, and in the West for the Recipient.

The Recipient shall say a short, earnest prayer to the Lord of all, in hopes of healing his affliction, and then take a seat. The Imhotep sits down, and instructs the Recipient. Firstly, the Recipient is told to apply the Oil to the body part corresponding to the force being used. If this ritual is meant to address a specific physical ailment, at this point the Imhotep will apply the poultice, or the Recipient will apply the Oil to the area being treated. The Imhotep always moves clockwise. Next, the Imhotep instructs the recipient to touch first his heart, and next the Image within the Book. (This is to set up the link between the recipient and the Image.) Now, the Recipient is to take up the cup (prepared with 3 ounces of the Unda Superum, and 3 ounces of distilled water) and with closed eye and receptive heart, drink the prepared Unda Superum. The Recipient replaces the cup on the Table. Now the Recipient is told to stare intently, with locked gaze, upon the Image. He is told to take seven slow, careful breaths, while concentrated upon the image, and then to sit down and close his eyes.

At this point, the Recipient is told to meditate upon the Image, holding it with his Inner Eye, whilst continuing the slow, measured breathing. After a period of twelve breaths, he is instructed to open his eyes, and to lock his gaze upon the eyes of the Imhotep. The Imhotep uses this gaze to create a strong connection. After a moment, the Recipient is instructed to close his eyes, and the Imhotep guides him through performing the Bellows-Breath, with concentration upon the heart.

After filling the heart with LVX, the Imhotep instructs the Recipient to sit in silent meditation for a short time, with the awareness placed upon the healing Image within the Book. The Imhotep, after instructing the Recipient about the Act of Thanksgiving, turns to face the East. He divests himself of the Godform Imhotep (Vibrating the name in silence) and then gives the Sign of Silence. He will wait in the adjoining room/outside for the Recipient.

THE ACT OF THANKSGIVING

The Act of Thanksgiving is the closing act of the Rites of Healing. Here, the Recipient kneels down, facing the east, and says a short prayer of Thanksgiving for the Healing he has received. It should be spontaneous and heartfelt. After finishing the Prayer, the Recipient may leave upon the table some token of his appreciation for the work of the Spagyrist Healer.

SO ENDS THE BOOK OF THE BLOSSOMING FLOWER.

PRACTICAL APPLICATIONS OF THE HOLY YEHESHUA RITE

CREATING SERVANT-SPIRITS

Creating servant-spirits is very simple once the Alchemist has a firm grasp of the Holy Yeheshua rite. The methods for creating a servant spirit in this system are straightforward, and of the nature of the Conjure Hand.

CREATING AN ELEMENTARY SPIRIT

A spirit meant to accomplish a task that is related directly to one of the Elements is created by using the Mudra and vibrating and the letter associated to the Element in the Holy Yeheshua Rite into existence.

Prepared before the ritual are the makings of a Spirit-Hand – red flannel bag, Angelica Root, a solid amount of a root or herb associated with the element, and a quartz crystal. The Angelica Root ensures spirit of a helpful nature, and the root/herb/curio of the Element gives it the Virtue it needs to accomplish the task. The quartz crystal is where I place the essence of the entity during the ritual, as a powerful symbol for Alchemical Salt and Coagulation – this is the spirit's rooting into the physical world to do its work. I use Red Pepper flakes for Fire, Ginger Root for Water, Rose Petals for Air, and Sea-Salt crystals mixed with loamy dirt from my yard for Earth. The quartz crystal is added to the bag at the end of the Rite, and then sealed shut. The bag should only be opened when the Alchemist is ready to release the entity and dissipate it back into the force from which it came.

While concentrating on the nature of the Force, the Alchemist repeatedly inhales it into the Sphere of Sensation until the Sphere is dense and vibrating with its power. The Alchemist then states the intent of the Work, and describes the Nature of the Spirit and what purpose it is made for. This is also written down on a name-paper beforehand (it is best to use a fine parchment). Recite the Elemental invocation as given previously for creating candle-engines, and then hold the Letter floating above in your awareness. Using your vision, shape the Letter into the form of a person, and then – continuing to hold it with your Mind – push it down into the crystal. Perform the Sign of Silence. Place the name-paper and the quartz into the Spirit-Hand, and tie the bag shut.

The hand must be fed a minimum of once a week, using a drop of whiskey or fine oil made for the purpose, and fumigating it with sweet-smelling incense. Speak to it daily and it will work for you. The spirit can be communed with using divination.

To dissipate the entity, open the spirit-bag and say "In the name of the Lord, I set you free." Pull out the crystal, and hold it under running water. Watch in your inner vision as the Letter within it fades away, and when it is completely gone, bury the crystal. Never re-use a crystal or the substance of a spirit-bag.

HOMUNCULI

Spirits can be created using combinations of the Elements in order to get specific effect from them; if all the of Elements – including Spirit – are included in the creation of the Spirit, then you have made a Homunculus of sorts which must be treated with a certain respect, as it is made in the image of Man. These should only be created for long term and deep need, or as lifetime companions. They cannot be simply dissipated, but can be set free to do as they will. They will develop their own wills, and can be difficult to control, just like people. Be careful when releasing one; do so carefully, binding it from doing harm, as its evil will be your own evil. We are responsible for what we create.

INVOKING THE ASTROLOGICAL FORCES

The elemental Mudra from the Holy Yeheshua Rite are used as Keys to open the temple space to the astrological force of the Sign. To do this, we invoke the forces of the Elements in a specific pattern when the Sign is rising in our location (free astrological software like ZET can help you determine this if you are not astrologically experienced). This pattern is the Key to the Astrological force, and we obtain this pattern from a Golden Dawn teaching about the 12 Banners of Israel. They are permutations of the Holy word YHVH, each of which is connected to a different Astrological Sign.

The Twelve Banners are as follows:

Aries: YHVh
Color: Red
Symbol: The Ram

Taurus: YHhV
Color: Red-Orange
Symbol: The Bull

Gemini: YvhH
Color: Orange
Symbol: The Twins

Cancer: HvhY
Color: Amber
Symbol: The Crab

Leo: HVYh
Color: Greenish Yellow (heavier on the green-side)
Symbol: The Lion

Virgo: HhVY
Color: Yellowish Green (heavier on the yellow-side)
Symbol: The Maiden

Libra: VhYH
Color: Emerald
Symbol: The Scales

Scorpio : VhHY
Color: Indigo
Symbol: The Scorpion

Sagittarius: VYHh
Color: Dark Blue
Symbol: The Centaur, drawing his bow

Capricorn: hYHV
Color: Blue
Symbol: The Goat

Aquarius: hYVH
Color: Violet
Symbol: The Man

Pisces: hHVY
Color: Crimson (reddish-purple)
Symbol: The Fishes (two fishes, swimming away from one another)

The color attributions are those that I have found efficacious, based loosely on the color wheel and the King Scale of the Golden Dawn's color-correspondences for the Astrological forces. They work; if my attributions are dissonant for you, use those with which you are familiar.

These are, of course, the English letters; in practice the letters should be formed in Hebrew.

What we have in these 12 Banners are an elemental key to unlocking pathways connecting us directly to the force of an Astrological Sign. By using our Mudra and their connection to the holy word YHVH, we can open this pathway and work with the forces of the Signs. The Twelve Banners rite given below can be used to connect with the Astrological Force, and then fill the Sphere of Sensation, a room or space, or a material basis for a talisman with the Virtue of the sign.

Summarized, the Twelve Banners rite first requires cleansing with the Purification Rite, and then invocation of the Astrological fore by using the Mudra to create the Key for it. The symbol of the Sign is then vibrated into existence by the Alchemist directly above the permutation of YHVH that he created, in the color appropriate for the Sign. Using pore breathing, the Alchemist pulls the LVX from the "realm" of the Sign into the Sphere of Sensation, or uses the loading breath (simply holding the Sign with the Awareness upon inhale, and flowing LVX from within the realm of the Sign into the room or talisman) to load the room or talisman with the virtue of the Sign.

THE TWELVE BANNERS RITE

1. Perform the Purification Rituals.

2. Perform the Holy Yeheshua Rite, filling yourself with power, raising and refining your nature.

3. Using one Mudra at a time (and visualizing the Letters while doing so, the same as when performing the Holy Yeheshua rite) create the Key for the Sign before you. The Letters should be formed from right to left, as they are Hebrew. They are written in order from left-to-right in this text's reference. The letters must be formed with strong vibration, but they must be visualized in the color appropriate for the Sign. For example, if invoking the force of Aries, all of the letters would be blood-red, and the letters would be formed thus 'hVHY', with Y been the first letter intoned.

4. Draw the symbol for the Sign (for Aries it would be the Ram) in the appropriate color for it directly above where you've created the Key. Use either your hand or the Wand of Imhotep for this. Intone its name as you do so. Using the Sign of the Enterer, project LVX into the symbol. You will immediately perceive its vibrancy and power, as the Sign becomes a Gate to the essence of the Astrological force, through the action of the Key.

5. Using pore breathing, inhale into your Sphere of Sensation the virtue of the Sign, perceiving it as light that is the color of the Sign, until your Sphere is in sympathy with it. If you are working to purify and balance your own portion of this force, be sure to especially focus on the LVX penetrating your physical body. Do so 12 times. Now, state what your intent is, what you wish to accomplish with the force.

6. If you wish to fill your temple with the force of the Sign, do the same as above, and then hold the sign in your Awareness. Upon inhale, focus intently upon the Sign and upon exhale allow the force to flow from the Sign out into the room or space. Continue with these breaths (called "loading" breaths) until the room appears 'full' to your inner vision and perception.

If creating a talisman, after performing steps 1 through 5, project the force into the Material basis using the Sign of the Enterer. Seal it within the basis using the Sign of Silence.

7. End the Rite (assuming it is the last working of the session, otherwise save the license to depart for later) by thanking and blessing the spirits and virtue involved in the work. Give them leave to depart, with instruction to return again at your call. Breathe in and out slowly, allowing the force to dissipate some with each breath, until it is gone from your vision.

THE MAGIC OF THE DECANS

THE HEALING MAGIC OF THE DECANS

We use the *Testament of Solomon* to discover the nature of these particular Spirits in order to work with the Decans for Healing. The *Testament* gives us a list of the Decan Spirits who have malefic influence on the lives of folk through illness of the body and mind; by summoning these Spirits and commanding them in the name of Sabaoth, we follow in the footsteps of Solomon and gain the power to exorcise them – and the illnesses they cause. You will find upon reading that many of the maladies that afflict us are given a Spirit we can work with, making this a fantastic tool for accomplishing healing at the root spiritual level. As given in the Book of the Blossoming Flower, healing an illness is best addressed as a multi-layered problem involving physical manifestation and spiritual root. Working with the Solomonic spirits of the Decans gives us a fantastic tool to do exactly that. It is also efficacious for those who don't have a grasp of Spagery, or perhaps don't have the temperament or funds to spend gaining skillful use of it.

It is important that the guidelines are followed strictly – no shortcuts when working with Spirits that cause painful maladies! The triangle *must* be made, as well as the Circle, and the Alchemist simply does *not* leave the Circle until after the license to depart is given, and the banishing incense burnt.

The Circle itself is simple but incredibly important. It is created using circumambulation – ritual movement in a circular direction – while intoning and drawing in the space before you Holy names of Saturn and of God. Saturn is used to bless and prime this circle because of his Ascendancy over the entire Zodiac in his aspect as AION in lore.

It is important to treat these entities with respect; they do the job that God, in its wisdom, determined they should do. They are not evil any more than a tornado is evil; that being said, a tornado does not need to be evil to destroy your home. It need only exist under inauspicious circumstance. These entities are, in one way, personified natural forces – in this particular case illnesses or maladies of the body. With this system of Evocatory magic, we first gain the ability to work with the entities, and to recognize their signature in the states of the body. Then, we use the technique given us by Solomon to free the body of them – buttressed by the techniques of Conjure. Hoodoo has a long tradition of working with the Grimoires; the natural magic of Hoodoo pairs quite nicely with the Spirit work.

OPENING THE TEMPLE

We open the Temple for this work by Invoking the Astrological Force to which the Decan is assigned, and then loading the room with it using the breath-based technique given in the previous section in the 12 Banners Rite. The elemental Mudra from the Holy Yeheshua Rite are used as Keys to open the temple space to the astrological force of the Sign within which the Decan resides. In order to do so, we invoke the forces of the Elements in a specific pattern during the time when the Decan is rising in our location (free astrological software like ZET can help you determine this if you are not astrologically experienced). This pattern is the Key to the astrological force, and we obtain this pattern from a Golden Dawn teaching about the 12 Banners of Israel. They are permutations of the Holy word YHVH, each of which is connected to a different Astrological Sign. To Open the Temple, perform the 12 Banners Rite for the Sign in which the Decan-Spirit finds its home.

CREATING THE TRIANGLE

The Triangle must be created before the Circle, as we are not leaving the Circle until after the Work itself is done and the Spirit departed. It is painfully stupid to do otherwise. The Triangle (with the apex pointing away from the Circle), should be made simply, of three candles dressed with Sweet Domination oil (recipe follows) which is made to sweeten the spirit and to keep it under the power of the Alchemist. They should be placed atop white ribbon (or chalk) that delineates the limits of the Triangle. The word AZOTH should be written upon parchment and placed at the center of the Triangle, over which the scrying Orb or mirror is placed. This alludes to the mystery of Khronos/Saturn whose cloak is the AZOTH, the fundamental Chaos from which all things spring, the Black Powder of creation. From this Chaos we will draw the image of the Decan Spirit. An incense of the Planet that rules the Decan should be burnt within the Triangle.

Sweet Domination oil is made simply: of John the Conqueror root, Sugar, a bit of Burdock Root, and Salt (to aid in manifestation). There should be far more John the Conqueror than Sugar, at least a two-to-one ratio. A naming paper explicitly describing the purpose of the oil should be placed within the jar that contains the oil. The natural virtue of the roots provide the power, the naming paper the direction. We use it to empower us, but for the yoke to be gentle.

CREATING THE CIRCLE

We are going to create a vortex with our movements within the boundaries of the Circle, at the center of which the Alchemist stands surrounded by and in Union with the name of God. This sort of circle works by moving the spiritual force that approaches it in a clockwise fashion (clockwise because that is the direction the Sun moves, and is balancing to un-balanced forces) through the power of the Holy Names before it reaches the Alchemist, who stands with God in the Center. Any force or current that attempts to penetrate the Circle is rendered harmless. It is important to create the Circle before communing with possible malefic entities, as it robes the Alchemist in the authority of the God under which the Spirits of the Decans serve, keeping the Alchemist safe from attack or malfeasance by the entity. Any unbalanced forces which touch the Circle are balanced when they reach the Alchemist.

Begin by facing the East, standing in the East of your temple room, at the outskirt (but within the boundary!) of where you want your circle to be. You should use a rope, cord, or chalk to delineate the boundary of the circle. (If you use rope or cord, be sure to tie the ends together so that it is truly a circle. It is not enough to simply touch the ends together.) The rope should be purest white in color, the chalk as well. First walk around the delineation of the circle (be it rope or chalk) with lit incense, incanting "In the Name of the Lord, YEHOVAH ELOHIM, this space is pure and Holy, and all within is Holy." Return to the East after censing the limits of the Circle. Vibrate deeply and powerfully, AION. Moving clockwise, walk to the South, then West, then North and finally back to the East of the room, standing about a foot behind where you were when you began (remember, we are creating a vortex, which is a spiral). Face the East, and vibrate deeply and powerfully, KHRONOS. Do the same again, ending in the center of your Circle. Vibrate deeply and powerfully, SABAOTH.

You've created the Circle, and are now ready to commune and command the Spirits of the Decans.

THE PROCESS

First Purification, then Open the Temple, and create the Circle and Triangle. State "In the name of the Lord SABAOTH, n. (where n. is the name of the Decan-Spirit), I command you to appear, willingly and in a form natural to you and un-offensive to the Mind." If you have done this work while the Decan of the Spirit is rising, it is there. It simply has no other choice, as the name of God SABAOTH commands it and the astrological timing ensures that it is there to receive your message. Take a moment to allow its image to rise in the mind's sight upon the Mirror or the scrying Orb. Ask it what its name is, and what its effects upon the body are. State that "As Solomon did before me, in the name of the Lord SABAOTH, I will do such-and-such, and your influence will retreat as given in the *Testament*." The spirit will concur. At this point, bid it farewell and thank it generously for coming. Command it to leave in the name of the lord SABAOTH, and burn the banishing incense, saying "HEKAS, HEKAS, EST BEBELOI". Declare the day's work to be finished. Burn the banishing incense on the censer (using plenty of burdock root). Do not leave the Circle until all of this is accomplished. Cleanse your Mirror or Orb with Holy Water, and cleanse yourself with the same.

Once you have done this with these spirits, you may use the techniques given in the *Testament* below to banish the illnesses caused by these entities. It is a truly useful Magic. If using this Magic to work upon someone distant, place a quartz crystal within the Triangle, and command the entity to transfer its influence upon "n". (where n. is the name of the afflicted individual) into the crystal. Bid him depart, finish the closing.

THE *TESTAMENT* EXCERPT, WITH PLANETARY RULERS AND THE BANNERS USED TO SUMMON THE DECAN-SPIRITS

Then I Solomon invoked the name of the Lord Sabaoth, and questioned each in turn as to what was its character. And I bade each one come forward and tell of its actions.

The First Decan of Aries
Planetary Ruler: Mars
Banner: YHVh
Name: Ruax
Angel/Action that imprisons it: MICHAEL

Then the first one came forward, and said: "I am the first decans of the zodiacal circle, and I am called the ram, and with me are these two." So I put to them the question: "Who are ye called?" The first said: "I, O Lord, am called Ruax, and I cause the heads of men to be idle, and I pillage their brows. But let me only hear the words, 'Michael, imprison Ruax,' and at once I retreat."

The Second Decan of Aries
Planetary Ruler: Sol
Banner: YHVh
Name: Barsafael
Angel/Action that imprisons it: GABRIEL

And the second said: "I am called Barsafael, and I cause those who are subject to my hour to feel the pain of migraine. If only I hear the words, 'Gabriel, imprison Barsafael,' at once I retreat."

The Third Decan of Aries
Planetary Ruler: Venus
Banner: YHVh
Name:Arotosael
Angel/Action that Imprisons it: URIEL

The third said: "I am called Arôtosael. I do harm to eyes, and grievously injure them. Only let me hear the words, 'Uriel, imprison Aratosael' (sic), at once I retreat."

The First Decan of Taurus
Planetary Ruler: Mercury
Banner: YHhV
Name: Mercury
Angel/Action Imprisons it: The text gives us nothing for this Decan.

The Alchemist is encouraged to discover the name and work of this entity on his own. Carefully.

The Second Decan of Taurus
Planetary Ruler: Luna
Banner: YHhV
Name: Iudal
Angel/Action that Imprisons it: URUEL IUDAL

The fifth said: "I am called Iudal, and I bring about a block in the ears and deafness of hearing. If I hear, 'Uruel Iudal,' I at once retreat."

The Third Decan of Taurus
Planetary Ruler:Saturn
Banner: YHhV
Name: Sphendonael
Angel/Action that imprisons it: SABRAEL

The sixth said: "I am called Sphendonaêl. I cause tumours of the parotid gland, and inflammations of the tonsils, and tetanic recurvation. If I hear, 'Sabrael, imprison Sphendonaêl,' at once I retreat."

The First Decan of Gemini
Planetary Ruler:Jupiter
Banner: YVhH
Name:Sphandor
Angel/Action that imprisons it: ARAEL

And the Seventh said: "I am called Sphandôr, and I weaken the strength of the shoulders, and cause them to tremble; and I paralyze the nerves of the hands, and I break and bruise the bones of the neck. And I, I suck out the marrow. But if I hear the words, 'Araêl, imprison Sphandôr,' I at once retreat."

The Second Decan of Gemini
Planetary Ruler: Mars
Banner: YVhH
Name:Belbel
Angel/Action that imprisons it: ARAEL

And the eight said: "I am called Belbel. I distort the hearts and minds of men. If I hear the words, 'Araêl, imprison Belbel,' I at once retreat."

The Third Decan of Gemini
Planetary Ruler: Jupiter
Banner: YVhH
Name: Kurtael
Angel/Action that imprisons it: IAOTH

And the ninth said: "I am called Kurtaêl. I send colics in the bowels. I induce pains. If I hear the words, 'Iaôth, imprison Kurtaêl,' I at once retreat."

The First Decan of Cancer
Planetary Ruler: Venus
Banner:HVhY
Name: Metathiax
Angel/Action that imprisons it:ADONAEL

The tenth said: "I am called Metathiax. I cause the reins to ache. If I hear the words, 'Adônaêl, imprison Metathiax,' I at once retreat."

The Second Decan of Cancer
Planetary Ruler: Mercury
Banner:HVhY
Name: Katanikotael
Angel/Action that imprisons it: ADONAEL, Iae, Ieo

The eleventh said: "I am called Katanikotaêl. I create strife and wrongs in men's homes, and send on them hard temper. If any one would be at peace in his home, let him write on seven leaves of laurel the name of the angel that frustrates me, along with these names: Iae, Ieô, sons of Sabaôth, in the name of the great God let him shut up Katanikotaêl. Then let him wash the laurel-leaves in water, and sprinkle his house with the water, from within to the outside. And at once I retreat."

The Third Decan of Cancer
Planetary Ruler: Luna
Banner:HVhY

Name: Metathiax

Angel/Action that imprisons it: Iaco, Iealo, Ioelet, Sabaoth, Ithoth, Bae

The twelfth said: "I am called Saphathoraél, and I inspire partisanship in men, and delight in causing them to stumble. If any one will write on paper these names of angels, Iacô, Iealô, Iôelet, Sabaôth, Ithoth, Bae, and having folded it up, wear it round his neck or against his ear, I at once retreat and dissipate the drunken fit."

The First Decan of Leo

Planetary Ruler: Saturn

Banner: HVYh

Name: Bobel

Angel/Action that imprisons it: ADONAEL

The thirteenth said: "I am called Bobêl (sic), and I cause nervous illness by my assaults. If I hear the name of the great 'Adonaêl, imprison Bothothêl,' I at once retreat."

The Second Decan of Leo

Planetary Ruler: Jupiter

Banner: HVYh

Name: Kumeatel

Angel/Action that imprisons it: Zoroel

The fourteenth said: "I am called Kumeatêl, and I inflict shivering fits and torpor. If only I hear the words: 'Zôrôêl, imprison Kumentaêl,' I at once retreat."

The Third Decan of Leo

Planetary Ruler: Mars

Banner:HVYh

Name: Roeled

Angel/Action that imprisons it: Iax

The fifteenth said: "I am called Roêlêd. I cause cold and frost and pain in the stomach. Let me only hear the words: 'Iax, bide not, be not warmed, for Solomon is fairer than eleven fathers,' I at once retreat."

The First Decan of Virgo
Planetary Ruler: Sun
Banner:HhVY
Name: Atrax
Angel/Action that imprisons it:

The sixteenth said: "I am called Atrax. I inflict upon men fevers, irremediable and harmful. If you would imprison me, chop up coriander and smear it on the lips, reciting the following charm: 'The fever which is from dirt. I exorcise thee by the throne of the most high God, retreat from dirt and retreat from the creature fashioned by God.' And at once I retreat."

The Second Decan of Virgo
Planetary Ruler: Venus
Banner:HhVY
Name: Ieropael
Angel/Action that imprisons it: Iudarize, Sabune, Denoe

The seventeenth said: "I am called Ieropaêl. On the stomach of men I sit, and cause convulsions in the bath and in the road; and wherever I be found, or find a man, I throw him down. But if any one will say to the afflicted into their ear these names, three times over, into the right ear: 'Iudarizê, Sabunê, Denôê,' I at once retreat."

The Third Decan of Virgo
Planetary Ruler: Mercury
Banner:HhVY
Name: Buldumech
Angel/Action that imprisons it: the Names as written below.

The eighteenth said: "I am called Buldumêch. I separate wife from husband and bring about a grudge between them. If any one write down the names of thy sires, Solomon, on paper and place it in the ante-chamber of his house, I retreat thence. And the legend written shall be as follows: 'The God of Abram, and the God of Isaac, and the God of Jacob commands thee – retire from this house in peace.' And I at once retire."

The First Decan of Libra
Planetary Ruler: Saturn
Banner: VhYH
Name: Naoth
Angel/Action that imprisons it: Phnumoboeol

The nineteenth said: "I am called Naôth, and I take my seat on the knees of men. If any one write on paper: 'Phnunoboêol, depart Nathath, and touch thou not the neck,' I at once retreat."

The Second Decan of Libra
Planetary Ruler: Jupiter
Banner: VhYH
Name: Mardero
Angel/Action that imprisons it: Sphener, Rafael

The twentieth said: "I am called Marderô. I send on men incurable fever. If any one write on the leaf of a book: 'Sphênêr, Rafael, retire, drag me not about, flay me not,' and tie it round his neck, I at once retreat."

The Third Decan of Libra
Planetary Ruler: Jupiter
Banner: VhYH
Name: Alath
Angel/Action that imprisons it: Rorex

The twenty-first said: "I am called Alath, and I cause coughing and hard-breathing in children. If any one write on paper: 'Rorêx, do thou pursue Alath,' and fasten it round his neck, I at once retire."

The First Decan of Scorpio
Planetary Ruler: Mars
Banner: VhHY
No other information about this Decan is available from the *Testament*.

The Second Decan of Scorpio
Planetary Ruler: Sun
Banner: VhHY

Name: Nefthada
Angel/Action that imprisons it: Iathoth, Uruel, Nepthada

The twenty-third said: "I am called Nefthada. I cause the reins to ache, and I bring about dysury. If any one write on a plate of tin the words: 'Iathôth, Uruêl, Nephthada,' and fasten it round the loins, I at once retreat."

The Third of Scorpio
Planetary Ruler: Venus
Banner: VhHY
Name: Akton
Angel/Action that imprisons it: Marmaraoth, Sabaoth

The twenty-fourth said: "I am called Akton. I cause ribs and lumbic muscles to ache. If one engrave on copper material, taken from a ship which has missed its anchorage, this: 'Marmaraôth, Sabaôth, pursue Akton,' and fasten it round the loin, I at once retreat."

The First Decan of Sagittarius
Planetary Ruler: Mercury
Banner:VYHh
Name: Anatreth
Angel/Action that imprisons it: Arara, Charara

The twenty-fifth said: "I am called Anatreth, and I rend burnings and fevers into the entrails. But if I hear: 'Arara, Charara,' instantly do I retreat."

The Second Decan of Sagittarius
Planetary Ruler: Moon
Banner:VYHh
Name: Enenuth
Angel/Action that imprisons it: Allazool

The twenty-sixth said: "I am called Enenuth. I steal away men's minds, and change their hearts, and make a man toothless. If one write: 'Allazoôl, pursue Enenuth,' and tie the paper round him, I at once retreat."

The Third Face of Sagittarius
Planetary Ruler: Saturn
Name: Pheth
Angel/Action that imprisons it: process as below

The twenty-seventh said: "I am called Phêth. I make men consumptive and cause hemorrhagia. ,If one exorcise me in wine, sweet-smelling and unmixed by the eleventh aeon, and say: 'I exorcise thee by the eleventh aeon to stop, I demand, Phêth (Axiôphêth),' then give it to the patient to drink, and I at once retreat."

The First Decan of Capricorn
Planetary Ruler: Jupiter
Banner: hYHV
Name: Enenuth
Angel/Action that imprisons it: Allazool

The twenty-eighth said: "I am called Harpax, and I send sleeplessness on men. If one write 'Kokphnêdismos,' and bind it round the temples, I at once retire."

The Second Decan of Capricorn
Planetary Ruler: Mars
Banner: hYHV
Name: Anonster
Angel/Action that imprisons it: Marmarao

The twenty-ninth said: "I am called Anostêr. I engender uterine mania and pains in the bladder. If one powder into pure oil three seeds of laurel and smear it on, saying: 'I exorcise thee, Anostêr. Stop by Marmaraô,' at once I retreat."

The Third Decan of Capricorn
Planetary Ruler: Sol
Banner: hYHV
Name: Alleborith
Angel/Action that imprisons it: method as below, and hilarious.

The thirtieth said: "I am called Alleborith. If in eating fish one has swallowed a bone, then he must take a bone from the fish and cough, and at once I retreat."

The First Decan of Aquarius
Planetary Ruler: Venus
Banner: hYVH
Name: Hephesimireth
Angel/Action that imprisons it: Seraphim, Cherubim

The thirty-first said: "I am called Hephesimireth, and cause lingering disease. If you throw salt, rubbed in the hand, into oil and smear it on the patient, saying: 'Seraphim, Cherubim, help me!' I at once retire."

The Second Decan of Aquarius
Planetary Ruler: Mercury
Banner: hYVH
Name: Icthion
Angel/Action that imprisons it: Adonaeth

The thirty-second said: "I am called Ichthion. I paralyze muscles and contuse them. If I hear 'Adonaêth, help!' I at once retire."

The Third Decan of Aquarius
Planetary Ruler: Luna
Banner: hYVH
Name: Agchonion
Angel/Action that imprisons it: Lycurgos, ycurgos, curgos, yrgos, gos, os

The thirty-third said: "I am called Agchoniôn. I lie among swaddling-clothes and in the precipice. And if any one write on fig-leaves 'Lycurgos,' taking away one letter at a time, and write it, reversing the letters, I retire at once. 'Lycurgos, ycurgos, kurgos, yrgos, gos, os.'"

The First Decan of Pisces
Planetary Ruler: Saturn
Banner: hHVY
Name: Autothith
Angel/Action that imprisons it: Alpha, Omega

The thirty-fourth said: "I am called Autothith. I cause grudges and fighting. Therefore I am frustrated by Alpha and Omega, if written down."

The Second Decan of Pisces
Planetary Ruler: Jupiter
Banner: hHVY
Name: Phthenoth
Angel/Action that imprisons it: Image of a weeping eye

The thirty-fifth said: "I am called Phthenoth. I cast evil eye on every man. Therefore, the eye much-suffering, if it be drawn... frustrates me."

The Third Decan of Pisces
Planetary Ruler: Mars
Banner: hYVH
Name: Bianakith
Angel/Action that imprisons it: Melto, Ardu, Anaath

The thirty-sixth said: "I am called Bianakith. I have a grudge against the body. I lay waste houses, I cause flesh to decay, and all else that is similar. If a man write on the front-door of his house: 'Mêltô, Ardu, Anaath,' I flee from that place."

This concludes the section on Practical applications.

For Further Alchemical Understanding – an analysis of Philalethes' *Font of Chemical Truth* from the perspective of the Ordo Octopi Nigri Pulveri.

I would encourage alchemists working with this system to read the following analysis and attempt to internalize the alchemical thinking of this Ordo. There are certainly other valid ways to interpret this and other Alchemical texts; understanding our methods will help you internalize our Alchemical system. When you have sufficient understanding of this, you can apply that understanding to other ancient Alchemical text, and derive further understanding about Internal Alchemy from them, regardless of whether they intended it so or not.

The sections italicized below are the words of Philalethes, with the analysis in regular type.

Sectional Analysis of the *Font of Chemical Truth*

"Our Magistery consists of three parts: the first deals with the essential and substantial composition of our Stone; the second describes their manner of combination; the third the mode of chemical procedure. Our substances are "red ore," or matured Sulfur, and water, undigested Mercury, or "white ore." To these a vessel is added, a furnace, and a triple fire. In discussing their manner of combination, we have to consider their weight and the regimen. The weight is twofold, and so is the regimen: between them they produce the following processes – Calcination, Dissolution, Separation, Conjunction, Putrefaction, Distillation, Coagulation, Sublimation, Fixation, and Exaltation. The first two produce the black, viscous powder, by means of the "unnatural fire," a temperate, incomburent, and altering ignition. There is then a further change into a mineral water. The three operations which follow are the result of the first and third fires, namely, natural and contra-natural, and "circulate" the substance, until the gross is separated from the subtle, and the whole is evenly tempered, the separated elements being then recombined, impregnated, and putrefied."

The nature and components of our Alchemical operations are here given by Philalethes. He defines the primary substances we work upon, the Red Ore that is the physical body/waking mind-personality, and the White Ore that is the Spiritual body/sub-conscious mind. He describes this as "undigested", meaning it hasn't been refined as of yet by alchemical processes. These substances are contained within the vessel, which is the Sphere of Sensation (aura). The furnace in which we contain and stoke the Heat is the physical body, which lies within and is inter-penetrated by the Alchemical Vessel. Often you will see in Alchemical emblems that the fire is shown to be within the glass vessel, although it is just as valid to place the fire outside of this vessel in the imagery, as the Sphere of Sensation penetrates within as well. The triple fire is the multi-natured fire we use to refine the materials – the un-natural fire brought in from without the sphere, which is the LVX/MANA/ORGONE/ENERGY... call it what you will... the Inner Fires that are contained within the nerve-centers represented by the metals, and the digestive fire, which must be tempered if the other fires are to have their way with the Prima Materia. We are told the "weight" is two-fold – this alludes to the dual nature of the Ores – and the "regimen" is two-fold; this refers to the work being both spiritual and Physical. In deep reality, there is only one matter, and this is understood after Dissolution. Practically, because of the Salt Force, we must work with what we can perceive, and that means acknowledging the separation of the Body and Spirit, which will become recombined in our Understanding.

In this interpretation of Philalethes' system, Calcination and Dissolution are the creation of the Black Powder by means of the "unnatural fire" – this is application of heat to the combined substance that creates the initial Change. Further alchemical meditation produces the mineral Water, so-called because it is infused with the powers of the "minerals" – the energetic nerve-centers that are our Metals, our Planets. This is done by making the body subtle, by applying "heat" to the body gently by filling it with the "unnatural fire", using the willpower and the breath. This done over time will provoke the Saturn force at the base of the spine to rise, destroying identification with the personality and creating the experience of the Black Powder. The next three steps are completed by use of the natural and unnatural fires; namely, the LVX applied as heat to the internal Metals, which give up their Vapor, their Inner Fires that are stored as nerve-energy within the Metals (Philalethes seems primarily to work with Mars, Saturn, and Jupiter directly) and the circulation and filling of the subtle and physical body with LVX through alchemical meditation (which is the un-natural fire, the spiritual fire).

Separation separates the Gross from the Subtle; this is perception of the subtle truth of a thing through meditation, the primary subject being ourselves, the First Matter. This is nature disrobing and revealing herself to the Alchemist. We sit in alchemical meditation, and observe the Self. The making-subtle of the bodies creates a state in which we can observe the First Matter, and, separating the Gross from the Subtle, the densely manifest and separate (through the action of Salt, the form making property) ethereal mind perceive it all for what it is truly made of Azoth, the stuff of God.

Conjunction is the re-unification of the Gross and the Subtle; this is the refined subtle body and mind penetrating and permeating the physical body. Again, this requires continued circulation of the Inner Fires, the Natural and Unnatural.

Putrefaction is the gradual Blackening of the Alchemist's bodies; this blackening is symbolic of the change in state that results from continued alchemical meditation and tempering of the bodies by the Inner Fires. This is a change in the make-up of the Alchemist, so that the truth of the Black powder pervades not just the mind and personality, but also the physical and energetic bodies. This is also the rising of the Death-Force found in Saturn, who eats the Alchemist and births him anew. The Salt Force holds less sway after this event, and the truth of Nature is ever available to the Alchemist's understanding.

"The five last operations are the result of natural fire which increases and gets stronger from day to day, purifying the putrefied substance of its dross, by continual ascensions and descents. This process is therefore called distillation, volatilization, ablution, imbibition, humectation of the earth, and is continued until the dryness gradually thickens the substances, and, finally, under the influence of coction or continued sublimation, induces fixation, the terminal point of which is exaltation, an exaltation which is not local, from the bottom to the surface, but qualitative, from vileness to the highest excellence.

These operations are sometimes called regimens; but there. are only two kinds of fire, the natural and the non-natural, the latter being employed to call out the activity of the former. Putrefaction precedes regeneration, *and is caused by the strife of the two fires. That part of the work which is subsequent to putrefaction and conjunction, when the Sulfur and the water have become one, and also receive congelation, is effected by the natural fire alone."*

What is said here is that the final steps of the operation happen by means of the circulations and the natural fire; that the fires held within the Nerve centers do the work on their own, as they are refined by the Alchemist's continued Calcination and Dissolution of the substance of the First Matter. There are no additional processes required from the Alchemist as far as operations go. The gentle application of "heat", of the Inner Fires, does the work. He also specifies that the work with the unnatural fire - the LVX - calls the natural fires into action. He goes on to say that the further stages are the result of the natural fires, the refinement of the individual Metals.

"The substances are our body (commonly styled Lemnian earth) and our water (our true rain water). Our water is the life of all things, and if you can by much toil obtain it, you will have both silver and gold. It is the water of Saltpetre, and outwardly resembles Mercury, while inwardly at its heart there burns purest infernal fire. Do not be deceived with common quicksilver, but gather that Mercury which the returning Sun, in the month of March, diffuses everywhere, till the month of October, when it is ripe."

Here he defines the substances that are joined and worked with as the refined Body of the Alchemist and His Gold-impregnated Mind (filled with the seed of Soul). He makes it clear that the "Water" is the life of all things; this is a reference to Soul, the seed of which is at the heart of all things that exist. Saltpetre, which literally translated means "Stone Salt", is an allusion to the Physical portion of the Philosopher's Stone, the refined Physical Body of the Alchemist. The "water" of this stone appears to be common Mercury - it appears to be common Mind - but the fire of ignited Soul burns within. His comments about Astrological conditions related to the Sun - the Solar Light that is the Gold and the substance of Soul - denote that the strength and availability of this Solar LVX is tied to the Sun's natural cycle. Lemnian Earth is our body, our Furnace - called Lemnian as an allusion to Vulcan, whose mighty forge was in Lemnos.

"Know that our Mercury is before the eyes of all men, though it is known to few. When it is prepared, its splendour is most admirable; but the sight is vouchsafed to none, save the sons of knowledge. Do not despise it, therefore, when you see it in sordid guise; for if you do, you will never accomplish our Magistery – and if you can change its countenance, the transformation will be glorious. For our water is a most pure virgin, and is loved of many, but meets all her wooers in foul garments, in order that she may be able to distinguish the worthy from the unworthy. Our beautiful maiden abounds in inward hidden graces; unlike the immodest woman who meets her lovers in splendid garments. To those who do not despise her foul exterior, she then. appears in all her beauty, and brings them an infinite dower of riches and health. Our Queen is pure above measure, and her splendour like that of a celestial being – and so indeed she is called by the Sages, who also style her their quintessence. Her brilliancy is such as baffles imagination, and, if you would have any idea of it, you must see it with your own eyes. Our water is serene, crystalline, pure, and beautiful- though it can assume its true form only through the aid of our Art. In that form it is our sea, our hidden fountain, from which gold derives its birth by natural descent; yet it is also stronger than gold, and overcomes it, wherefore gold is united to it, and is washed in it, and the two together grow up into a strong hero, whom neither Pope nor Emperor can buy for a price. Hence you should, above all things, seek this water, by means of which (with the solitary addition of a clean and perfect body) the Stone may be prepared."

Here Philalethes expounds on the virtues of the Purified Mind, which is only available to the "sons of knowledge"; those who study and meditate. The mind that is revealed through the Separation of the Gross and the Subtle, the true mind that is like a Black sea within us and available to all who look deeply enough, and enriched by the congealed Vapor of the inner Fire released from the metals, particularly the Jupiter center. We are all born with a Mind we value (loved by many), deceived into grossness by the Salt force. He advises us not to despise it for its vulgarities, or we will never accomplish the Magistery of refinement of the Mind and growth and multiplication of the Soul within us. He describes the nature of the true Mind/Spirit. He chooses words that re-enforce the Internal nature of this Mercury; saying that our maiden abounds in "inward hidden graces". To those who continue to Observe her – who meditate upon her – and don't "despise" or turn away from her, but continue to behold her (meditate upon her) she appears in all her beauty. This is a reference to the Separation, where, having circulated the fires and sat in meditation, the observed Mind is perceived as it truly is. The Mind, when its clothing of Personality is thrown off (these are the foul garments) is one point of light in the Sea of Lights that is the Azoth, the body of God. He states that if you want any idea of it, you must see it "with your own eyes". This means that the revelation of the nature of Mind is something experienced; reading alone will not reveal it. He further goes on to describe the Mercury as the sea, and as the hidden fountain from which Gold is born. Gold – Soul-matter – descends from the Heavens (the seed within grows, the lady Mercury is "impregnated") into the prepared bodies of the Saltpeter and True Mercury – the refined Body and refined Mind.

> "But it requires profound study to become acquainted with all the secrets of our sea, and with its ebb and flow. It took me 18 months, after I had discovered the spring of our water, to find the method of making it well forth, because I did not know the meaning of the fiery furnace of the Sages. When I discovered it, indeed, the sight which I beheld richly rewarded me for all my pains. I was then suddenly, as by a flash of inspiration, enabled to understand all the secret words and enigmas of the Sages. Our water is the fire which causes both death, and, through death, a more glorious life. Whoever discovers it has reached the autumn of his Magistery, as Nature will then (when the pure body has been put into it) perform all the other processes, and carry the substance onward to perfection through all the different regimens. This water, though one, is not simple, but compounded of two things: the vessel and the fire of the Sages. and the bond which holds the two together. So when we speak of our vessel, and our fire, we mean by both expressions, our water; nor is our furnace anything diverse or distinct from our water. There is then one vessel, one furnace, one fire, and all these make up one water. The fire digests, the vessel whitens and penetrates, the furnace is the: bond which comprises and encloses all, and all these three are our Mercury. There are many kinds of fire (and of water) in our Magistery, but all these only represent different aspects of our Mercury."

The Spring of our Water is the universal mind, the Azoth, the body of god. He then goes on to speak of our water, which is our mind/Etheric body. He goes on to speak of the Nature of the First Matter, which is truly Mercury as it is manifest on different levels of existence, all held within the person who is like the image of God. Just as the Metals are congealed Mercury, so is the body itself. All matter is Mind; there is no separation, only the illusion of such as created by the Salt-force, which gives form and structure and separateness. There are many different Fires; just as there are many different individuals with different qualities. In the end, at their root, they are all Mercury. The Vessel is the Sphere of Sensation, and the Fire of the Sages the Gold, the Soul, the infernal and hottest of the Inner Fires. It spreads through Multiplication and sets the entirety of the Alchemist's bodies alight.

> "There is only one thing in the whole world from which our Mercury can be obtained. It is like gold in essence, but different in substance, and if you change its elements you will have what you seek. Join heaven to earth in the fire of love, and you will see in the middle of the firmament the bird of Hermes. Do not confound the natures, but separate and re-combine them, and you will reign in honour all your life."

The one thing from which Mercury can be obtained is the Body. It is fundamentally the same as Gold, made of the Sun and Solar fire (we are made entirely of Solar energy; the plants we consume derive their sustenance directly from the Sun, and the Animals from those plants. We are Solar creatures, through and through, and so are made of Gold, but un-refined Gold.). Refining this body is changing its elements. Joining Heaven to Earth in the Fire of Love is done through use of the Inner Fire found within the Venus center, in the throat. This Fire is in sympathy with the love-force that pervades nature. When this center is awakened and refined with the bellows-breath, the fire rises as the Eagle. This center is at the Gate, the spiritual joining-point of the various bodies. Use the un-natural Fire to stimulate this Center, and you see within the "Middle Firmament" which is the mind's eye (between the Heavens and Earth), the bird of Hermes. This Bird is the Eagle, the subtle vapor that ascends from the Metals. We are to separate the Natures via meditation. Immersing them in the Waters of Mercury, we will see that at root they are one and the same. This moment of revelation accompanies the combining of the two natures.

"In the South-west there is a high mountain (very near the Sun), one of seven, and the second in height This mountain is of a very hot temperature (because it is not far from the Sun), and in this mountain is enclosed a vapour or spirit, whose services are indispensable for our work. But it does not ascend, unless it is quickened, nor is it quickened unless you dig knee-deep on the summit of the mountain. If you do this, a subtle exhalation (or spirit) ascends, and is congealed by the air into drops of beautifully limpid water – which is our water, our fire, our vessel, and our furnace; not common Mercury, but the hot and moist liquid of most pure Salt, which we call Mercury, because in comparison with the Sun, it is immature and cold. If the Almighty had not created this Mercury, the transmutation of metals would be impossible, because gold does not tinge unless it be first tinged itself. Our Mercury is the beloved spouse of gold, and changes its body into a purely spiritual substance; gold loves it so, that for very love he dies, and is revived by his spouse, and she is impregnated by him, and conceives, and bears a most beautiful royal son. The whole knowledge of our Art consists in the discovery of this our sea; any Alchemist who is ignorant of it, is simply wasting his money. Our sea is derived from the mountain of which I told you above. The exhalation or white smoke which ascends there, will accomplish our whole Magistery."

This begins by associating Mountains (which are projections from the Earth, and the Earth is our Body) with the Seven Planets. This particular "mountain" – Planet – is close to the Sun. We know the Sun is located in the Chest above the Heart, as the nerve-center above Heart. This mountain, then – this Jupiter – is located within the body below the Sun center, at the Solar Plexus. Digging "knee deep" means to work with the Planet within the Earth. The Earth, which is the physical body, contains the Mountain. Digging is instruction to reach within the body to stimulate and quicken the Planet, which will release a "vapor", a subtle exhalation. This vapor is a subtle internal fire; it is called a vapor because it is subtle and it rises up toward the heavens (to the Alchemist's head). It is perceived within the Body in feel as a rising invigoration, moving from the Solar Plexus into the Head, which throbs in sympathy. The stimulation by un-natural fire causes the Inner Fire that resides in the Planet to rise up and do its good work.

The beautiful limpid water is the substance of purified Mercury; after the Eagle (vapor, inner Fire) rises from the Jupiterian center it condenses into this, which becomes the stuff that all of our bodies are composed of. Pure salt – Saltpeter, the purified and thoroughly calcined body – emanates a new and purified personality and spirit... a golden Child, a revitalized and holy Self. Just as our impure Salt, our mature Red Ore, has created and emanated a personality for us (built of the bodily experiences the Person has had), so will the refined Alchemical body emanate a Self. The change is a gradual one, but a fixed and permanent one. The seed of Gold, of Soul, kept within us and distributed through the Metals, "dies", is transformed into the subtle vapor that impregnates the Mercury, our subtle mind and spirit, which then is transmuted into the nature of this Soul. Instead of being endlessly reborn, as a Seed that becomes a Tree, which then gives seed and is reborn again, the Alchemical Soul/Seed creates the immortal Person of its own substance, one who can exist within the Halls of God without endless rebirth.

"There is another secret which you should know if you wish to see your hope fulfilled, viz., how you are to dig a hole in the mountain, as its surface is impenetrable to ordinary tools, its dryness being such that it has become harder than a flint. But in the places of Saturn a small herb is found, called Saturnia, whose twigs appear dry, but in whose roots there is abundance of juice. This herb you should carefully take up with the roots, and carry with you to the foot of the mountain, and, with the help of fire, bury it beneath the mountain; its virtue will at once penetrate the whole mountain, and soften its earth. Then you may ascend to the summit, easily dig a hole knee deep, and pour in so much dry and viscous water, that it penetrates to where the herb lies buried, and makes it ascend as a fume, which carries upward with it the spirit of the mountain. This spirit is the strength of fire mingling with water, and dwelling in it. The spirit of Saturnia is the whitening fume, the vapour of the mountain is fire, and all these things are fire. Thus you obtain Saturnia, the royal plant and mineral herb, which together with fat flesh makes such a soup as to eclipse the richest banquets in the world. Here is an enigmatic description of our water, which should in course of time and study, become plain to the diligent enquirer. There is the King (gold), and the water which is the King's Bath; our water is the vessel, inasmuch as our King is enclosed in it, and the furnace, inasmuch as our fire is enclosed in it, and our fire, inasmuch as the virtue or spirit of the mountain dwells in it, and the woman, inasmuch as it receives the vapour of the plant Saturnia; and as the dear friend of the Sun penetrates, whitens, and softens it, and *causes it to emit its sperm. Then the fiery virtue which is in the water, begins to act on our body, wasting and mortifying it, until at length the innate heat of the Sun is roused into activity. Our Stone is called a little world, because it contains within itself the active and the passive, the motor and the thing moved, the fixed and the volatile, the mature and the crude – which, being homogeneous, help and perfect each other. We have already shewn that our object in adding matured Sulfur to crude Mercury (the same thing in different stages of development), is to shorten and accelerate the natural process. Gold is a hot and dry body, silver a frigid and humid one, Mercury the means of conveying tinctures. The body of the Sun is most highly digested, that of the Moon imperfect and immature, while Mercury is the bond by which these two contraries are united. Join the Moon to Mercury by means of proper heat, so that the two become one Mercury which retains its inward fire; then the Mercury will be freed from all dross and superfluities, and it will become transparent like the tears we shed, though not exactly perspicuous. If you then unite this purified Mercury to gold, in which is the Moon and fire, the hot and dry will love the cold and humid, and they will unite on the bed of the fire of friendship; the man will dissolve over the woman, and the woman be coagulated over the man, till the spirit and the body become one by commixtion. Continue the same operation (let the heaven descend to the earth) till the spirit puts on the body, and both are fixed together. Then our Stone will have obtained its royal virtue. For Mercury is the water of all metals, and they are digested in it. When vegetables are boiled in ordinary water, which is naturally frigid and humid, it partakes of their qualities, and is yet separable from them; so the pure Mercury, which is in all metals and minerals, is perfectly separable from the dross and foreign matter which has become mixed up with them; yet the different minerals and metals qualify the Mercury in the same way as the water is qualified by the vegetables cooked in it. There are these two differences between the Mercury and the water, that the water is not coagulated and fixed with the vegetables as our water is with the metals; and that, while the colour of common water is changed by anything boiled in it, Mercury retains its own colour and fluxibility, though its essence is qualified. Therefore the Mercury is effectual in the dissolution of the metal, and the metal in the coagulation of the Mercury; and as, in the dissolution, the form and colour of the metal is latent in the form and colour of the Mercury, so, in coagulation, the form and colour of the Mercury is hidden* in the form and colour of the metal; neither do the qualities of the metal in dissolution prevent the fluxibility of the Mercury, nor the qualities of Mercury in coagulation the fixity of the metal. Do you not here observe a wonderful harmony between Mercury and the metals? For their love is like that of mother and son, sister and brother, male and female. Hence they are calculated mutually to perfect each other, the water imparting to the body a spiritual and volatile nature, while the body gives to the water a corporeal substance. The reason that the colour of Mercury is not changed in coction by the dissolved body, is this: the earth and water in the Mercury are homogeneous, and so well tempered that neither can be separated from the other, and they are so well mixed that the whole substance exhibits (together with great fluxibility) so great a consistency as entirely to conceal the colours – and only if a part of the Mercury is destroyed or marred by some deleterious chemical corrosive, are the colours seen. The relations of Mercury in respect of earth and water are these: in respect of water it is fluxible and liquid, in respect of earth it moistens nothing but what is of the same essence with it. These hints will enable you to detect any errors in your treatment of Mercury. Some obstruct or divide its homogeneity by unduly drying up its water; others corrupt the earth and render it diaphanous by disproportionate mixing. Mercury is the sperm of the metals; it contains in itself the Sulfur by which alone it is digested (through which Nature would in course of time have matured it into gold); nor would it be possible to convert Mercury into gold without it. This mature Sulfur, then, is radically mixed with the Mercury, and rapidly digests it, while itself is putrefied by the Mercury, and is revived again, not as common, but as spiritual, penetrative, and tinging gold, which has power to purify imperfect metals of all their dross, and to change them into its own nature. Thus you see that none of the Mercury should be destroyed, or violently dealt with; all you have to do is to add to it a mature body sprung from the same root, and mix the two in their smallest parts, by means of our cunning conjunction (which is performed, not by a manual, but by a purely natural process, of which the Artist does not even understand the cause). We must distinguish, however, between our transmutative conjunction, and a sort of conjunction practised by sophists which is merely a fusing together of the two substances, and leaves each exactly what it was before. In our operation the spirit of gold infuses itself into the spirit of Mercury, and their union becomes as inseparable as that of water mixed with water. The conjunction can take place only by means of the Moon or an imperfect body and fire; and this Moon is the sap of the water of life, which is hidden in Mercury, and is stirred up by fire; it is a spirit which enters the body, and compels it to retain its soul. We speak not of common Mercury (which lacks the spirit and fire), but of our Mercurial water – though common Mercury may be made like it by the addition of that which it lacks. Our conjunction is the grand secret of our Art for earth is not inseparably united to water, but the union of water with water is indissoluble; hence our conjunction can take place only after dissolution, which dissolution takes place through the Moon and fire that are in the Mercury. For the Moon penetrates and whitens, and the fire mortifies and frets, while water combines both these properties, according to the philosophical dictum: "The fire which I shew you, is water," and, "Unless the bodies are subtilized by fire and water, nothing can be done in our Magistery." Thus everything, from beginning to end, is accomplished, not by sophistical operations, but by our Mercury, which, unless it be violently impeded, is kept to the right road by the necessity of arriving at a certain goal."

The final section begins with instruction on how to make the body subtle, so that the various metals may be reached and stimulated into releasing their vapor – which congeal in the head into pure Mercury, Mind/Spirit. We are told to go to the foot of the mountain; this is the base of the Torso/Perineum, where the Saturnian nerve-center is located. This is the "herb" Saturnia, and its twigs – the nerves – appear to be dry, to be fully solid. They have subtle roots within the body, however. They have an abundance of "juice". Just as liquid vivifies a plant, and carries the life-force, so does the Inner Fire, which vivifies the Metals in the body, carry the life-force. We are to "take up" the Saturnia by the roots... that is, hold it in our awareness, and place that awareness deep within our own mountain, at the perineum where the Saturn center lies. We are to apply heat to the herb, a gentle fire. This is the un-natural Fire, the LVX. We fill the center with the LVX slowly and regularly, in meditation. As the Metal heats, its Inner Fire rises and penetrates the Bodies of the Alchemist, rendering them subtle. This is a key Fire, one of the Triple, the Blackening Flame.

www.ingramcontent.com/pod-product-compliance
Lightning Source LLC
Chambersburg PA
CBHW070044100426
42740CB00013B/2791